THE PRIVATISATI(

Andy Croft's books include *Red Letter Days, Out of the Old Earth, A Weapon in the Struggle, Selected Poems of Randall Swingler, After the Party, Forty-six Quid and a Bag of Dirty Washing, Bare Freedom* and *The Years of Anger*. His plays include two Edinburgh Festival Fringe productions, *Smoke!* (2004) and *Horty Porty* (2005). Writing Residencies include the Great North Run, the Hartlepool Headland, Middlesbrough Town Hall, the Southwell Poetry Festival, the Combe Down Stone Mines Project, the Teesside Transporter Bridge, HMP Holme House and HMP Moorland.

Also by Andy Croft

Contents

ISBN: 978-1-916938-67-0

Cover designed by Aaron Kent

Cover art © Design Couple / Adobe Stock

Typeset by Aaron Kent

Broken Sleep Books Ltd
PO BOX 102
Llandysul
SA44 9BG

there is an absolute incompatibility between art and private property.
— John Berger, *Permanent Red*

The long game. Unlimited billy goats gruff.
And always, always only one troll.
— Wayne Holloway, *Our Struggle*

in memory of Cliff Cocker, Morning Star arts editor 2010–21

The Privatisation of Poetry

Andy Croft

Broken Sleep Books

INTRODUCTION

Awards! They always give out awards! I can't believe it. Greatest Fascist Dictator: Adolf Hitler...

— Alvy Singer, *Annie Hall*

In my first week at Nottingham University in 1975, the writer Stanley Middleton came to talk about his novel *Holiday*. Eager to meet a 'real writer' for the first time, I arrived at the event early – but found myself completely unable to go through the door, somehow feeling that I did not have the right to enter. British society is very good at persuading people to think that we are not allowed in, that culture belongs to others who are better qualified by class and money and culture and geography and education.

Much of my working life over the last forty years has been spent trying to hold the doors open as widely as possible for others who want to step inside – in university adult education, in schools, prisons and community projects. I have worked in over 400 schools and a dozen prisons; for ten years I edited a weekly column of readers' poems in the Middlesbrough *Evening Gazette*; I ran the Writearound Community Writing Festival in Cleveland (1989-2000), the T-junction International Poetry Festival in Middlesbrough (2014-18) and the Ripon Poetry Festival (2017-24); I wrote a monthly poetry column in the *Morning Star* from 2004-22, and for many years edited the 'poem of the week' feature in the paper. I helped run Teesside community-publishers Mudfog Books from 1993 to 2003, since when I have edited Smokestack Books. For the last six years I have been one of the judges of the Culture Matters annual Bread and Roses poetry competition sponsored by UNITE. The essays and reviews in this book can only be understood in this context.

I have chosen to reprint these pieces out of the several hundred book-reviews I have written since 1980, because they express a kind of developing argument with the world of British poetry – specifically regarding issues of access, privilege and ownership.

During that time large sections of British economic life have been moved out of common ownership into private hands, rationed by price or simply closed down. The democratic process is blocked by inequality, authoritarianism, deceit and a narrow ideological consensus. British cultural life is blocked by the values of big business and show business.

The result is an atomised, unwelcoming and unfriendly poetry scene whose inaccessibility is hardly disguised by ritual declarations about diversity and inclusion. Conversations about poetry have been replaced by conversations about poets, discussions of tradition by accusations of plagiarism, and the language of literary criticism by the language of press-releases promoting corporate prizes and celebrity book-festivals. As Mark Fisher once put it, 'all that is solid melts into PR':

> Over the past thirty years capitalist realism has successfully installed a "business ontology" in which it is simply obvious that everything in society... should be run as a business... conditioning not only the production of culture but also the regulation of work and education, and acting as a kind of invisible barrier constraining thought and action.

Jonathan Davidson has called this the 'poetry-industrial complex', a tightly controlled market in which high-profile prizes 'help select the most profitable lines of investment' for corporate publishers:

> Competitions generate the cannon fodder of the perennially disappointed, while providing the industry with its national heroes. Slim volumes are barely read but are a useful means of stoking the fires of ambition for the unpublished and are also a means of creating value through scarcity, a scarcity that is further inflated through a prize culture.

The US poet Amanda Gorman was recently invited to chair the New York Met Gala (together with singer Billie Eilish, actor Timothée Chalamet and tennis-player Naomi Osaka). Photographed by Annie Leibovitz for the cover of *Vogue*, Amanda Gorman is now an Estée Lauder 'global changemaker'. Meanwhile, the National Poetry Library in London recently hosted an exhibition 'Poets in Vogue', of clothes worn by famous twentieth-century poets – a skirt worn by Sylvia Plath on a visit to Paris, a kaftan like one worn by Audre Lorde after her mastectomy, a red dress like one sometimes worn by Anne Sexton at poetry readings. This feels like a door that is still firmly locked.

Today there are only three kinds of poet: 'Prize-winning Poet', 'Emerging Poet' (hasn't yet won a prize) and 'Rising Poet' (hasn't yet published a book). A few years ago, when I gave a series of readings in the US, I was embarrassed to find that I was introduced everywhere as an 'award-winning English poet'. What other kind could there be? Juliana Spahr and Stephanie Young have described the North American system of poetry prizes thus:

> Some days we think of poetry as a dead antelope and poets as wolves, hyenas, and cayotes who come to fight over the innards, teeth bared, growling. Some days we think of poetry as the centre panel of Bosch's *Garden of Earthly* delights with poets as the naked libertines in small groups that notice only each other, some immersed in a pool balancing apples on their heads, some floating together in a bubble, others riding on the backs of birds.

The essays in this book were written in the belief that poetry is essentially a public and collective expression of emotionally shared symbolic meanings. The word 'symbol' is derived from the Greek word *symbolon*; in ancient Greece, two friends sharing hospitality would break a piece of pottery in half, each keeping one piece as a token of friendship and recognition. The critic Byung-Chul Han has argued that the writing and reading of poetry is itself a kind of ritual of social exchange:

> According to the myth related by Aristophanes in Plato's *Symposium*, humans were originally globular beings with two faces and four legs. Because they were so unruly, Zeus sought to weaken them by dividing them in two. Ever since their division, humans have

11

been *symbola*, longing for their other half, longing for
a healing wholeness.

A poem is an exchange of factual and emotional and imaginative information. It is also a potential exchange of trust, vulnerability and kindness. The writer of a poem has to trust that strangers will treat kindly their best attempt to express, describe, imagine and understand the world. The reader has to trust that the writer will treat them kindly by helping them to make sense of and enjoy a poem that they have never seen before. Each relies on the other's understanding that this exchange is both difficult and important. Writers and readers have to listen to each other carefully. But it is increasingly hard to hear anything against the constant white noise of PR and hyperbolic praise competing for ownership over the Next Big Thing.

The poet Randall Swingler once put it like this:

> It must always be remembered that poetry is older and simpler than any other form of language. It fulfils, in fact, the original function of language, intended by its rhythmical character to keep people together, to organise their powers into a unity, to make them aware of their common nature and interest, their essential community one with another... as imagination is the primary function of the mind so poetry maintains the primary function of language, of stimulating social activity in persons engaged together in a common task. Hence the reaping-songs, and the sea-shanties, the ballads and the early epics, which are all of war, religious rites or navigation, the only activities which the group still pursued as a unity. The simplicity of poetry is the concrete force of its symbols: and so, much of modern verse-writing, since it does not subserve this primary function, cannot be classed as poetry at all... a different art, if you like, but not poetry. The art perhaps of correspondence or the art of games, which may be witty, pathetic, ingenious, sentimental, within the limits of those arts. Whatever poetry is, it is not a magpies' nest... What has happened to poetry then? Simply that in a profit-making society there is no place for it, where all social functions are

increasingly divided into individual specialization, and
the function of poetry is gradually eliminated.

Poetry is a way of knowing ourselves and others better, of sharing and extending the common ownership of experience, feeling and language, of resisting the forces that would divide us. Poetry is a social production or it is nothing at all. It is not a competition. It is not a career. It is not private property. Poetry belongs to everyone, not just to those with an agent, a back-story, a Creative Writing MA, a shiny prize and an Instagram following. The doors still need kicking down.

— *North Yorkshire 2024*

ANDY CROFT

REVIEW OF JAMES FENTON, *OUT OF DANGER*

The publication of *The New Poetry* and Linda France's *Sixty Women Poets* has marked a shift in cultural authority away from London, at least in the world of poetry publishing. Counter-canonical, both anthologies of course immediately became canonical. Which London publisher would have had the courage – or the authority to publish *Klaonica*? And for all Bloodaxe's success, Neil Astley remains part of the small press world, recently publishing full-length collections by poets such as Brendan Cleary, Ann Sansom and Geoff Hattersley, all of whom have been around the small press scene for several years.

This is the real achievement of Bloodaxe and the rest, to have legitimised the creative aspirations of a generation of writers who – for reasons of geography, experience and education – might otherwise have had to wait a very long time to be published by Faber or Chatto. And by doing this, they have alerted metropolitan poetry publishing to the possibilities of poetry written a long way from London (consider the way that Faber poached Simon Armitage after the success of *Zoom!*) The New Generation project may be understood as a clumsy attempt by corporate publishers to get back in on the act as if they were somehow equals.

Of all the recent efforts to seize the initiative from the North, the most notable has been the reinvention of James Fenton, who has reappeared with a new collection to declare, 'we despise the deformed, uncandid class conscious points. North for instance, does not mean good.'

Fenton was recently elected Professor of Poetry at Oxford, where as a student he was a Newdigate Prize winner. A former theatre critic for the *Sunday Times* and chief book reviewer for *The Times*, he is now a columnist for *The Independent*. A Fellow of the Royal Society of Literature, he won the Geoffrey Faber Memorial Prize for *The Memory of War*, while *Out of Danger* is a Poetry Book Society Choice. Fenton has been called 'the most talented poet of his generation' and the heir to Auden. The *New Yorker* has recently called him 'the greatest poet in all England.'

'Big titles, James. How did you win 'em?' asked Adrian Mitchell in the *New Statesman,* challenging Fenton to a poetry reading, the winner (by acclamation of the audience) to take 70% of the purse and the title of 'the greatest poet in all England.' So far Fenton has resisted the challenge. 'I'm not going to stand up in public and have Adrian Mitchell hurl insults at me,' he wrote in *The Independent.* 'If he thinks he can make himself the greatest poet in England in this way, I'm not going to help him out.'

It's not that Fenton's chicken (though Mitchell calls him the 'Oxford Professor of Poultry'). Just possibly the title isn't his in the first place. There are many better poets with better claims than his. Mitchell places Fenton 45th in the batting averages. Reading *Out of Danger*, however, even this seems over-generous.

This slim volume is his first book for ten years, 'eagerly awaited' (by Penguin at least), although many of Fenton's friends will already have read most of these poems which have apparently been published in a privately printed volume. It contains just twenty-three poems (three and a half in Tagalog), thirteen songs from a 'pocket musical' performed in Paris in 1990, and an odd assortment of *obiter dicta.* Some are simply trivial ('A Poem Against Barn Owls'), or silly ('On a Recent Indiscretion by a Certain Fullbright Fellow in Upper Egypt'), while others are so brief they sit at the top of an empty page full of an importance they do not have ('An Amazing Dialogue', 'The Poetry of Pure Fact').

There's nothing wrong with short, trivial or silly poems, particularly if you have a talent for the Audenesque. But Auden's reputation was built on rather more than this. And even the 'shorts' in Auden's early work combined a small, playground voice with some big and international subjects ('Pick a quarrel, go to war, / Leave the hero in the bar. / Hunt the lion, climb the peak, / No-one guesses you are weak.')

These are arguably the most important lines Auden wrote in the early 1930s, a key to his developing ideas about masculinity and 'The Truly Strong man'. As a former foreign correspondent, Fenton is also interested in the relationship between the private and the public, the individual and History. And at times he strains for this kind of effect – 'Tiananmen / Is road and clean / And you can't tell / Where the dead have been'. But the weak pun 'tell' is undone by the next lines 'And you can't tell / What happened when / And you can't speak / Of Tiananmen'. But where Auden was addressing a generation growing up to the temptations of the *Fuhrer-prinzip*, Fenton is talking to himself, a poet who writes a poem called 'Tiananmen' about the impossibility of writing a poem about the events in Tiananmen. As a result, the poem never rises above the simplicity of its manner, a kind of banal hand-wringing which tells us only that the Chinese Government was to blame for the killings – 'The cruel men / Are old and deaf / Ready to kill / But short of breath.' This is about as useful and as interesting as being told in 'A German Requiem' that the consequences of Nazism are unforgettable because we try to forget them, or in 'Cambodia' that a great many people died in Indo-China.

Saying the unsayable in blunt and direct rhyme was something Auden learned in part from Brecht, another poet with whom Fenton as been compared. Certainly, some of his songs reach for a Brechtian simplicity ('Blood and Lead') but they lack Brecht's knack of turning an everyday phrase on its head and shaking out of it economics, politics and common-sense. Compare, say, 'Brecht's 'Deutsches Miserere' or 'Song of the Nazi Soldier's Wife' with Fenton's 'Out of East' – 'A foreign soldier came to me / And he gave me a gun / And the liar spoke of history / before the year was done.' The potential force of the simple diction is undone by the use of the word 'liar'.

Where Auden and Brecht gave big statements to small people, looking at History through the wrong end of the telescope, Fenton gives us a kind of leader-writer's poetry ('Jerusalem'), big statements using big and abstract words. Comparisons with Auden and Brecht are made partly because Fenton's poems sometimes read like popular song lyrics from the 1940s ('Stay true to me and

I'll stay true to you – / As true to you are new to me will do, / New as the rainbow in the spray / Utterly new in every way, / New in the way that what you say is true.' But while a facility to write good/bad song lyrics may have earned Fenton a fortune (he provided some never-used lyrics for *Les Miserables*), this hardly makes him 'the greatest poet in all England' at a time when so many others have joined poetry to cabaret, rap, rock and jazz in those 'deformed, uncandid class conscious compass points' outside London.

— *Scratch* no 12, Winter 1994-5

SOME RESPONSES ARE MORE EQUAL THAN OTHERS

*There can never be common ground for those who believe that you
have to learn how to think and how to read before you can write and
those who think that poetry is just a response to experience and that all
responses are equal.*
— David Kennedy, *Thumbscrew 13*

'Most people', as Adrian Mitchell once famously put it, 'ignore
most poetry because most poetry ignores most people.' This is of
course regrettable, but at least it means that 'most people' don't
realise the contempt with which they are regarded by so many
poets. Contemporary British poetry is not so much a game which
everyone can play as an elite sport played by professionals to
which the rest of us are invited as spectators. It is a stately home
nature-trail patrolled on every side by game-keepers. It is a night-
club with more bouncers than dancers. It is a world in which,
according to Jane Holland in *Poetry Review*, 'there are too many
people out there writing poetry' – an opinion which subsequent
correspondence in the magazine suggests is 'the private view of
most serious poets' and editors 'who have to wade through oceans
of substandard verbiage on a regular basis to find anything worth
publishing.'

Although the new director of the Poetry Society, Christina
Patterson, says in the latest issue of *Poetry News* that the society
exists 'for poets, poetry lovers and those whose experience of
poetry consists largely of half-remembered poems at school', the
new issue of *Poetry Review* contains a rather different version of 'a
premier league of best-selling poets and the rest probably selling
somewhat fewer books than they did before the boom' (although
we are reassured that 'every now and then a poet will be promoted'
into the premier league). These two versions of the 'poetry revival'
are clearly incompatible. Poetry is indivisible. It either belongs to
everyone or it is not poetry but something else – show business,
self-advertising, big business fashion, marketing, retailing, self-
display. Poetry may appear to be the most easily available literary

form for most people (easier to write than a screen-play, easier to publish than a novel). But visitors are not always welcome in the Republic of Poetry, where citizens are treated as subjects and its borders are heavily policed.

Between what might be called the BSkyB/Old Trafford vision of poetry and the poetic equivalent of the view from the terraces at Chester City, lie a number of contradictions, unresolved questions about the role of poetry in British cultural life. On the one hand, poetry is an utterly marginal economic activity (representing less than 1% of UK book sales). On the other it is a key component of 'English Literature' (itself the bearer of special cultural authority since the 1920s). It is an increasingly important means of delivering national policy agendas (literacy strategies, reluctant-readers, non-traditional learners, part-time degrees etc), and yet compared to journalism, fiction, copy-writing or screen-writing it is the least clamorous, the least glamorous and the least powerful of contemporary literary forms. It is a source of light-hearted news stories for the broadsheets (the exciting extra-marital affairs of Hugo Williams and Craig Raine, the Laureate sit-com, the Hughes/ Plath mythopoeia etc) and yet it struggles to command attention in the review pages. Every year we celebrate National Poetry Day to the sound of literary magazines closing. In the Northern Arts region alone we have lately lost *The Echo Room, Iron, The Page, Panurge, Poetry Durham, Red Herring, Scratch, Tees Valley Writer* and *Writing Women*. The result is the dramatic return of poetry as spectacle, as an object of cultural consumption (World Book Day, National Poetry Day, the Whitbread, Forward, Eliot and National Poetry prizes, *The Nation's Favourite* cds etc) where the popularity of poetry is measured by sales returns and not by the number of people who are writing and publishing poetry. In this context, the demise of *Slow Dancer* represents a much more serious blow to the contemporary poetry scene than the decision of OUP to close its poetry lists (except that other publishers' lists are now silting up with refugees from OUP). Promotions like Poetry Places and The

Year of the Artist hardly compensate for the recent disappearance of so many provincial magazines, presses and alternative bookshops any more than reprinting already-published poems in the *Guardian* and the *Independent* makes up for the loss of Adrian Mitchell's weekly page of new verse in the *New Statesman*). Meanwhile, the triumphant restoration of metropolitan culture and the dumbing of commercial publishing and book-selling continue to narrow the points of entry to poetry.

Curiously the 'poetry revival' has done little to increase access to the writing of poetry, for all the talk of heteroglossia, of decentring cultural authority and attending to marginal voices. The New Gen promotion now looks like an unsubtle attempt by London publishers to regain ground lost to Bloodaxe in the previous decade. The new Penguin Modern Poets feels increasingly like the establishment of a new canon, with all the implied sense of a settled argument, or a selection defined by what and whom it excludes. *Poetry Review* is now arguably more canonical and more partisan than at any time in its history. Editor Peter Forbes finds room in *Scanning the Century* for Wendy Cope but not for Hugh MacDiarmid, for Sophie Hannah but not for Edward Thomas, for Glyn Maxwell but not for John Masefield, for Don Paterson but not for Edward Thompson, for James Fenton but not for Robert Bridges.

This is a culture happy to reproduce itself, effortlessly recycling the self-confirming judgements of publishers and the London prize-giving circuit, as it establishes the criteria which set 'professional' poets apart from their audience. Consider, for example, Forward Prize-winner Carol Ann Duffy's 'Dear Writer-in-Residence':

> Dear Writer-on-Residence, I enclose my verse
> (94 poems) it's three weeks' work.
> I'll call in next week, which is time enough
> For you to read, digest and admire the stuff...
>
> ...I don't know your work – I haven't much time
> To read modern poets and I bet it doesn't rhyme.
> But I hope, as a professional, you won't plagiarize
> Any of my best lines. (A word to the wise!!)

The hapless would-be poet doesn't have a clue. They also don't have a chance. How could we not sympathise with the professional writer-in-residence who has to deal with so many tiresome amateurs? Compare 'In Residence: A Worst Case View' by another Forward Prize-winner, Sean O'Brien. Included in *HMS Glasshouse* (which earned its author an E.M. Forster Award), it is another hymn to the relationship between poets-in-residence and their students:

> Here is the notice you put on the board
> And these are the students beating a path
> From their latest adventures in learning to spell
> To a common obsession with Sylvia Plath.
>
> Soon there are Tuesdays, long afternoons,
> Letting them tell you what's good about Pound.
> You smile and you nod and you offer them tea
> And not one knows his arse from a hole in the ground.

O'Brien's *Ghost Train* includes another end-of-residency valediction, 'Never Can Say Goodbye', which salutes all those who 'send ad infinitum / Truckloads of your latest works. / I wonder why you write 'em –':

> Because you write but never read,
> Because you never listen,
> Because you are the porcelain
> The caught-short Muses piss in.

Peter Reading goes one better in *Stet*, providing examples of the poetry written by all these hopeless amateur poets who write but never read and never listen. His 'Poem of the Week slot (10 quid prize)' is won by either dour 'McDonald (Mrs). Aberdeen' ('£10 to you, Mrs McDonald, for your very good poem') or 'Contented of Telford, Mrs'. Unsurprisingly, they are not Reading's most memorable work:

> All this terrible rape and murder
>   And mugging and violence galore
> And poor little children beaten
>   Oh! my heart can stand no more.

There is always someone on strike
    For better pay and terms,
Is there no end to this misery?
    No one ever learns.
But before despair descends
    Upon my sad head
A name crops up in the paper
    And I no longer wish I was dead!
I'm filled with fresh, new hope,
    I'm certain that Billy Graham,
With words of Truth and Love,
    Will bring an end to this horrid mayhem.

It is a highly effective strategy, an ironic take on Reading's own inability to see the wood from the trees, one of the sentimental, amateur, self-condemning (and crucially demotic) voices with which he justifies the book's misanthropic clichés ('Doesn't he ever write about *happiness*?'). But it is also an extraordinarily revealing moment of misogyny and old-fashioned snobbery.

As it happens, I edit a regular, weekly column of readers' poems in Middlesbrough's *Evening Gazette*. Since 1989 I have published well over a thousand poems in the paper, by readers young and old. Because the column is so popular, and because I receive so many poems each week, the paper also publishes a twice-yearly magazine of readers' poems. Much of the material comes from local schools, from creative-writing courses, writers' groups and refugees from accredited adult education. Several contributors have since been published by Teesside poetry publishers Mudfog Press, and many of the region's best-known poets have also appeared in the *Gazette* (notably Mark Robinson, Norah Hill, Maureen Almond, Gordon Hodgeon, Bob Beagrie and Pauline Plummer). But the vast majority live well beyond the institutions of education, poetry and publishing. Most submissions are untyped; they are sometimes badly-spelled and often ungrammatical; many rely on second-hand phrases and second-hand ideas; few suggest any familiarity with contemporary poetry. They are generally notable for what they do not say and do not know how to say, and are characterised by a limited range of poetic models. They are intensely personal but curiously anonymous at the same time, what Roland Barthes called 'writerly' texts. And of the tens of thousands of poems submitted over the last eleven years I cannot say there have been no sentimental, weak or poorly articulated poems.

But they are not all like that, not all of the time. The majority are well-crafted, understated little poems about the things that poems need to be written about – friendship, love, loss, hope, death, dismay, loneliness, disappointment. They are variously serious, silly, fierce, witty, uptight, solemn, funny, disbelieving, direct, sarcastic, sad, vehement and tender. Some set out to celebrate, others to question, to denounce, praise, remember, challenge, entertain, scare, glorify, shock, criticise, ridicule, hint, complain, shout, whisper and giggle. In other words, for all their limitations, these poems do what all poetry must do. And how could it be otherwise? Their authors are human; language is one of the ways we share and identify our experiences as human; poetry is a function of human society; we inhabit the same island, the same language, the same history. The poems published in the *Gazette* do not require a different kind of reader or a different kind of critical response. The issue, as always, is whether a poem is good enough, whether it is as close to what it is trying to say as it can be.

The impulses that lead people to write this kind of poem, to write it down and send it out, are no different, no worse, no less interesting or less admirable than the impulses that lead better-educated and better-read poets to sit down to write. Considering the huge barriers between 'most people' and poetry, the fact that so many still write it should be a source of amazement and admiration (how deep a common human impulse it must be) rather than disgust. For if there are technical and intellectual limits to this kind of poetry, they are simply an expression of the educational, political, economic and cultural processes for which Class is a clumsy but still necessary short-hand. For this is working-class poetry at the beginning of the twenty-first century. Of course, it is neither class-conscious nor politically militant. But then English working-class poetry has rarely been either (and at the beginning of the century the ex-industrial working-class is certainly neither class-conscious nor politically militant). The great virtue of working-class poetry is that it is unacquainted with postmodernity and unbound by the obligations of irony. Poets who live so far from the centres of cultural authority can thus address plainly subjects – war in Rwanda, Bosnia and Kossovo, the impact of heroin on local estates, ecological disaster in the North Sea, the treatment of pensioners by the present government – which 'better' poets can only approach via the most oblique and ironic routes. No event ever brought so many poems into the *Gazette* as the fall of Thatcher.

Poetry is popular. It always has been. It is just the buying of poetry books that's not so popular. Anyway, the *Evening Gazette* sells 70,000 copies a night, giving these working-class poets a rather larger readership than most poets ever dream of reaching. 'Most people' do not ignore poetry, no matter how much it ignores them. Most of us find ourselves at some time in our lives reaching for the heightened language and memorable phrasing, the economy of expression and patterned music that we call poetry. If we are in the middle of a genuine poetry revival, it is taking place in schools, community-centres and libraries, in writers' groups and creative-writing classes. It is sometimes written in private and often in secret. It is published on web-sites and on hospital waiting-room notice-boards, by small presses, in school magazines and in unhealthily slim volumes, in valentine-cards and *in memoriam* columns, in fanzines, in vanity-anthologies, parish magazines, local newspapers and trade union journals. It is performed at slams and open-mike slots, at leaving parties, wedding receptions and christenings, and sung to guitars and drum machines.

Contemporary poetry has clearly been enriched by listening to kinds of writing which, for reasons of ethnicity, race and gender, struggled until recently to find an audience. But a 'polycentred' literary culture must attend to the writing of working-class people too, to the poorly educated and the not so articulate, to the sometimes derivative, and the not always original. If we do not, then (like devolution or the London mayoral election) the 'poetry revival' will look increasingly like an exercise in disenfranchisement disguised as a widening of the franchise.

Poetry *is* a community, inhabited by everyone who has ever tried to write it. Forget Premier League football. If you want to promote poetry in terms of sport, I suggest that half-marathon running is a rather more useful metaphor. Every year over 40,000 people take part in the Great North Run. At the front there are a handful of élite athletes competing for a place at the Olympics. But not far behind them are tens of thousands of people who are running for almost as many reasons – to beat their personal best time, to improve on last year's time, to support a mate, to win a bet, to prove something to themselves, to impress friends or family, to lose weight, to raise money for charity, to get fit, to be as good as they can be. For most it is enough just to take part. You don't have to be fast or fit or clever or good-looking or well-educated to have a go, just as you don't have to want to win the Nobel Prize to start writing. Half-marathon running, like writing poetry, is a naturally democratic activity. It is about participating, not just watching. You don't need any qualifications to enter, no one is bothered about the medals, and the Olympians at the front don't mind sharing the day with the rest of us. Maybe it's time more professional poets joined in.

— *Thumbscrew* no 16, Summer 2000

MAGIC, MIMESIS AND MIDDLESBROUGH

Poetry is indispensable – if only I knew what for.

— *Jean Cocteau*

There was the poet who broke someone's nose in a fight before the reading (and who announced after the reading that he wanted a woman). There was the poet who was too drunk to begin the reading (and several who had drunk more than was good for them by the end). There were the poets who never turned up, the poet who forgot to get off the train, the poet who demanded a dressing room, and the poet who played his harmonica instead of reading any poems. There was an *alfresco* performance of a new version of *Beowulf* by the local Viking Society, and a fight between two Slammers broadcast live on the Internet. Meanwhile there were the pigeon-fanciers who arrived one night with their baskets of birds looking for a *poultry* reading...

Teesside is a long way from the centres of cultural authority (several well-known poets have refused the invitation to read so far from London). Nevertheless, by the late 1980s the informal development of a national network of live poetry events had extended even to the banks of the Tees. By the early 1990s there was an annual community writing festival (Writearound), a monthly poetry venue (Poetry Live!, later called the B[uz]z), performance venues (the Bare-Faced Cabaret, later the Verb Garden), and a twelve-month calendar of readings, performances, open mike slots, slams and book launches (and a wake to mark the demise of *Scratch*) in pubs and clubs, schools and colleges across Teesside. Middlesbrough even had its own annually-chosen poet laureates.

Almost all the most distinguished poets of our time have read in Middlesbrough during the last fifteen years – Carol Ann Duffy, Douglas Dunn, Tony Harrison, Liz Lochead, Adrian Mitchell, Carol Rumens, Ken Smith. There were some well-known combinations too – Simon Armitage and Kate Clanchy, Kathleen Jamie and Bill Herbert, Linda France and Paula Meehan, Jo Shapcott and Paul Farley, Don Paterson and Michael Donaghy, Selima Hill and Glyn

Wright, Henry Normal and Lemn Sissay, John Kinsella and Tracy Ryan. There were the two Brendans (Kennelly and Cleary), the two Matts (Simpson and Sweeney) and a Double Bill (Scammell and Herbert). The most frequent performer was Linda France, who read in Middlesbrough on six separate occasions, followed by Ian McMillan and Simon Armitage (four) and Brendan Cleary, Katrina Porteous and Keith Armstrong (three). Jackie Kay, Linda France, Katrina Porteous, Helen Kitson, Matthew Francis, Anne Rouse and Gillian Ferguson all read in Middlesbrough before their first collections were published.

Shoe-string funding means that readings are dominated by British poets, but wherever possible the programme includes writers visiting or temporarily resident in the UK and whose work speaks to different experiences, languages and cultures – Kamau Brathwaite (Barbados), Esiabi Irobi (Nigeria), Jack Mapanje (Malawi). Sudeep Sen (India), Charles Mingoshi (Zimbabwe), Fred D'Aguiar (Guyana), Freddie Macha (Tanzania), Kenneth Koch, Peter Plate and Jack Hirschman (USA). Punjabi and Urdu poets came from all over the UK to read at Teesside's annual *musha'ara*, Sam Milne read in Gaelic, Vladimir Druk read in Russian; Bill Griffiths and Clive Fencott read different poems at the same time, while MC Jabber performed at such speed it was hard to tell what language he was speaking.

Poorly-funded poetry readings in the back rooms of pubs in Middlesbrough may not signify much in the larger story of the current Poetry Revival; the 150 poetry readings which took place in Middlesbrough during this period were no doubt untypical of many significant national trends. Nevertheless, they shared a number of recurring features, enough at least to suggest some tentative observations on contemporary British poetry.

First, there is not an audience for live poetry. Rather there are several different and discrete audiences. During the 1980s and early 1990s, the poetry audience in Middlesbrough was typically composed of amateur writers and would-be poets, rather than the teachers and graduate professionals who constitute the natural audience for arts events elsewhere. While there was always a strong relationship with adult students on Leeds University's Creative-writing programme on Teesside, none of the English Department staff from Teesside Poly (now University) attended any live poetry readings in Middlesbrough in over a decade. Visiting poets regularly commented on the unusually attentive character of their audience – earnest and encouraging, keen to learn, critical, not easily distracted by celebrity or reputation.

Although this constituency has been seriously eroded by the subsequent 'mainstreaming' of adult education, it has been replaced, at least in part, by new and very different audiences – performance-poetry fans, Slammers and their supporters, children for whom poetry is a form of licensed freedom from SATs, as well as readers mobilised only by poets whose names reach well beyond the world of poetry (Hegley, McGough, Patten etc). The largest audiences at Poetry Live! were for Tony Harrison (85) and Douglas Dunn (70); the Verb Garden regularly attracts over 100 (mostly undergraduates) for readings in a local night-club ; the best-attended Writearound event was for the launch of a book of poems by local children (250); the Teesside *musha'ara* once attracted an audience of over 400; the largest recorded audience for a poetry reading in Middlesbrough (possibly in the UK) was at the Riverside Stadium where Mark Robinson once read to an audience of over 30,000 Boro fans before a game. But these are wholly separate sub-cultures. The reasons why people attend poetry readings are many and various and probably contradictory, and are only ever partly to do with poetry, never mind a consistent commitment to all kinds of poetry. There is almost no overlap between audiences whose expectations of poetry are often antithetical if not antagonistic. The first time Brendan Kennelly read in Middlesbrough it was to an audience of over 100 – almost all of whom were there anyway for the launch of an anthology by local poets.

Second, contemporary poetry is as atomised and as individuated as its audiences. Sean O'Brien's image of poets fighting like ferrets in a septic tank at least implies the continued existence of the tank.

And yet it is difficult to describe such different readings as those by O'Brien and say, Attila the Stockbroker, or Jane Holland and Apples and Snakes, or Maggie Hannan and Gordon Wardman, as sharing any lingering sense of a collective poetic tradition. Poets – like so much else in British life – must find their niche in the cultural market. This represents a significant weakening of what George Thomson once described as poetry's function as a shared, tribal, social activity:

> Art was not an individual but a collective production, although the first characteristics of individuality began to declare themselves tentatively in the sorcerer. Primitive society meant a dense, close-knit form of collectivism. Nothing was more terrible than to be cast out of the collective and to remain alone. Separation of the individual from the group or tribe meant death; the collective meant life and the content of life. Art in all its forms – language, dance, rhythmic chants, magic ceremonies – was the social activity *par excellence*, common to all and raising all men above nature and the animal world... the language of poetry is essentially more primitive than common speech, because it preserves in a higher degree the qualities of rhythm, melody, fantasy, inherent in speech as such... And its function is magical. It is designed to effect some change in the external world by mimesis — to impose illusion on reality.

Significantly, this sense of poetry as social ritual and magic may still be felt at Teesside's annual *musha'ara*, marathon poetry-readings in Urdu, Punjabi and English. Featuring up to ten poets and usually lasting four hours, the *musha'ara* always attract several hundred people of all ages. Instead of a fee, the poets are invited afterwards to a slap-up meal (heavily disguised in the budget) where the poetry continues to flow. The most distinctive feature of the *musha'ara*, however, is the level of audience participation – poets (who often sing their verses) are interrupted by applause, by requests for a line to be read again, by the audience guessing the rhyme at the end of a couplet or by joining-in during well-known poems. This is a collective, shared poetry, the expression of a literary, linguistic and religious identity among a community whose first language is English, but whose first *literary* language is Urdu.

According to Victor Kiernan, Urdu was originally a language of exile, the *lingua franca* of the nomadic camp:

> Verse forms and metres, besides diction, have helped to preserve continuity; and, still more strikingly, a common stock of imagery, which can be varied and recomposed inexhaustibly in much the same way that Indian (and Pakistani) classical music is founded on a set of standard note-combinations (*ragas*) on which the performer improvises variations.

Needless to say, very few non-Urdu speakers ever attend the *musha'ara*, and few Urdu poets go to readings at the B[uz]z or the Verb Garden (one who does so is clearly uncomfortable with most contemporary poetry, which he cannot connect to the English poetry he once learned at university). Although there are always a couple of English-only poets on the bill at the *musha'ara*, they are usually received with a strained and bewildered politeness. Those aspects of contemporary British poetry which are usually considered to be its characteristic virtues – irony, abrasiveness, moral relativism, comic eroticism, linguistic play, fleeting epiphanies, the poet as exotic traveller, the juxtaposition of trash cultural references with High Culture, the worship of the miniature and of the everyday – these seem to the *musha'ara* audience to have nothing at all to do with poetry. The only poets who have ever really been able to address this audience in its own poetic terms are Brendan Kennelly and Paula Meehan, two poets with an ear for tradition and a fabulous sense of rhythm and music, and who both recited rather than read; Paula Meehan's 'Lullaby' and Brendan Kennelly's rendering of songs by Patrick Kavanagh are still talked about at the *musha'ara*.

However – and third – the ability to address large and necessary subjects through a common, shared, emotional human music is a rare one. Too many contemporary poets do not always seem know to whom they are talking, or why. Not a few prize-wining poets misjudge the Middlesbrough audience by simply reading some poems, rather than inviting the audience to share in their work. This is not simply a matter of chatty asides between each poem, although some introduction to most poems is usually appreciated (Fred D'Aguiar once explained a poem at such length that he decided there was no point in reading it). It is not a question of 'performance' (some of the most hollow and lifeless readings have been by poets who believe themselves to be 'performance poets'). Nor is it simply a question of comedy. Many of the most vivid readings – by Arnold Rattenbury, Ian Crichton-Smith, John Lucas, Deryn Rees-Jones, Dorothy Nimmo, Bill Scammell, Mogg Williams, Neil Astley, John Longden, Mairi MacInnes – have been notably unfunny occasions of intense, concentrated seriousness. Some of the most celebrated poets have proved the least interesting readers. Some of the most successful readings have been by Teesside poets like Maureen Almond, Bob Beagrie Norah Hill, Gordon Hodgeon, Val Magee and Pauline Plummer, because they knew (and not just in a literal sense) to whom they were talking and why. The enviable traditions of Urdu poetry illustrate Christopher Caudwell's argument that poetry can be a means of returning to our original, common humanity:

> poetry is characteristically song, and song is characteristically something which, because of its rhythm, is sung in unison, is capable of being the expression of a collective emotion. This is one of the secrets of 'heightened language'... Unlike the life of beasts, the life of the simplest tribe requires a series of efforts which are not instinctive, but which are demanded by the necessities of a non-biological economic aim - for example a harvest. Hence the instincts must be harnessed to the needs of the group festival, the matrix of poetry, which frees the stores of emotion and canalises them in a collective channel... Thus poetry, combined with dance, ritual, and music, becomes the great switchboard of the instinctive energy of the tribe.

Fourth, poetry is an unexplained source of potential magic, through which we strive to impose our will on the world by mimicking the natural processes we wish to bring about. As speech is metaphorical, poetry is doubly so, the gift of Prometheus *and* Orpheus. Poetry-readings show poetry in movement, and reveal poets in relation to their audience in a way that no amount of close textual readings can do. When poets stand up to read in public, they have to address the readers beyond the page, the listeners across the room and beyond. According to Morris Zapp, in David Lodge's novel *Changing Places*, the act of reading is as unsatisfying as watching a striptease:

> The vagina remains hidden within the girl's body, shaded by her pubic hair, and even if she were to spread her legs before us... it would still not satisfy the curiosity and desire set in motion by the stripping. Staring into that orifice we find that we have somehow overshot the goal of our quest, gone beyond pleasure in contemplated beauty; gazing unto the womb we are returned to the mystery of our own origin. Just so in reading. The attempt to peer into the very core of a text, to possess once and for all its meaning, is vain – it is only ourselves that we find there, not the work itself.

In these terms, the potential pleasures of live poetry are not so solitary, unsatisfying or onanistic. In performance, poetry is a means of communication rather than a means of expression. It can clarify, focus, channel and release emotional and imaginative energy. It can connect poets to readers, and readers to poetry; it can send people home at the end of the evening feeling a little more connected to each other than usual. Inspiration, improvisation, prophecy and possession – these are the elements of what Ernst Fisher called 'the *necessity* of art':

> The magic at the very root of human existence, creating a sense of powerlessness and at the same time a consciousness of power, a fear of nature together with the ability to control nature, is the very essence

of all art. The first toolmaker, when he gave new form to a stone so that it might serve man, was the first artist. The first name-giver was also a great artist when he singled out an object from the vastness of nature, tamed it by means of a sign and handed over this creature of language as an instrument of power to other men. The first organiser who synchronised the working process by means of a rhythmic chant and so increased the collective strength of man was a prophet in art. The first hunter who disguised himself as an animal and by means of this identification with his prey increased the yield of the hunt... all these were the fore-fathers of art.

Several of the most memorable readings in Middlesbrough – notably by Bill Herbert, Adrian Mitchell, Brendan Kennelly, Simon Armitage, Ian McMillan and Matt Simpson – may be said to have shared this sense of ritual and music, of poetry as public property. Sebastian Barker introduced his poetry as a species of religious exaltation, while Kamau Brathwaite invited the West African god Shango to be present in the room during his reading. Like the *musha'ara*, many of the most successful readings have combined poetry and music – Katrina Porteous reading *Wind an' Wutter* accompanied by Northumbrian piper Chris Ormston, Linda France declaiming *Storyville* to an improvised jazz accompaniment, Pete Morgan and cellist Tony Moore, Labbi Siffre alternating poems and songs, John Harvey backed by jazz combo Second Nature. On one unforgettable occasion, the band 'Teeth like Razors' had a packed bar joining in the *Alabama Song* as an encore to a stunning performance of poetry and songs by Brecht. Magic.

Unfortunately, the idea of poetry as a form of shared social magic is not often found in contemporary British poetry. But then contemporary British poetry is not much of a community. The decline in poetry's music is hardly compensated for by a sudden access of 'sassiness' or 'edginess'. There is no longer a recognisable 'we' on this poor island; it is hard to write in the second-person plural, unless speaking on behalf of a private group or from within a specific relationship. The consequences of this are serious, both for poetry and for the society which it inhabits. As Randall Swingler (whose poetry once filled the Albert Hall) once put it:

> Poetry can and should sing and shout, in the open air, in the theatre, in the concert hall. Poetry also whispers and murmurs, around the fire or in the ear of a single person. It depends entirely upon what community the poet feels himself to share, and to press around him, at the time of utterance. If he feels himself to be alone and isolated, he will talk to himself, and it will probably sound like gibberish.

— in Mark Robinson (ed) *Words Out Loud* (Stride, 2002)

OFF WITH THEIR HEADS

In his farewell editorial in *Poetry Review*, Peter Forbes recently suggested that 'one unforseen consequence of New Generation was the creation of a new poetry aristocracy, a few of whom came to adopt an arrogant "we-are-the-masters-now attitude", seen at its worse [sic] in the denigration of Andrew Motion... and in subsequent attacks on this magazine for refusing to treat them as *Hello* treats the Beckhams.'

It's a tantalising passage (who *does* Forbes mean?) It's certainly an unexpected comment from the editor of the magazine that did so much to promote the New Generation. 'Seven Years On' from the New Gen campaign, *Poetry Review* recently 'took the pulse' of contemporary British poetry, showcasing the eighty-six 'most productive and creative poets today'. It's an impressive list of course, from Armitage to Zephaniah, New Gen, not-so-New Gen and well beyond. But it's not half so impressive as the list of poets who are absent – including Tony Harrison, Douglas Dunn, Gillian Clarke, John Lucas, Linda France, James Fenton, Geoffrey Hill, Edwin Morgan, Katrina Porteous, Matt Simpson, Sebastian Barker, Christopher Logue, Linton Kwesi Johnson... And this extraordinary *salon de refusé* of post-New Gen outsiders also contains, of course, hundreds of poets with only one book to their name, thousands with a couple of pamphlets, and tens of thousands more for whom writing poetry is an important but only occasional, and perhaps private, pleasure.

All this is a gorgeous footnote to New Labour Britain, where celebrity, public life and the arts meet in a gucci and sushi culture of glittering prizes and metropolitan marketing campaigns (everywhere beyond the M25 was described in a recent Arts Council document as the 'hinterland'). Seven years of New Gen poetry, five years of New Labour and three series of Big Brother. Blair's Babes and the intake of 1997 crowd the back-benches, New Labour peers troop into the House of Lords and the New Gen poets fill the pages of *Poetry Review*. It's a kind of post-Modern version of the Glorious Revolution, decorated by a newly-ennobled literary aristocracy, upwardly-mobile, bullish and not always on message.

Meanwhile poetry publishing – thanks to Waterstones and the collapse of the Arts Council-funded small-press distribution network – is in such serious crisis that even Bloodaxe have announced a three-year freeze on accepting first collections. As *Poetry Review* warns, 'a poetry world in which a few star poets swanned around and no new ones were coming forward would be a bit like a Royal Family *sans* an aristocracy: top-heavy and riding for a fall'. Those aristocrats again, only now they are required to sustain and protect the literary institutions and values enthroned at the centre. This sounds more like 1660 than 1685. Or perhaps a Cool-Britannia version of the court of Versailles, with the Poet Laureate as *le Roi du Soleil*. It's an extraordinary model for the world of contemporary poetry, which says a good deal about the relationship of the Poetry Society to both poetry and society. And what about the rest of us? What walk-on part do we get to play in this low-budget historical costume-drama?

The US poet Tom McGrath once said there were three kinds of poet. Recalling his Dustbowl Dakota childhood, he categorised poets into Cattlemen, Sheepmen and Outlaws. The first were those like Eliot and Yeats, 'aristos' who articulated a vision of the past with which to criticise the present; the second, like Whitman, Crane and Ginsberg, represented the literary equivalent of the rising bourgeoisie, open to all kinds of language and forms, old and new; the third were those like Neruda, Rimbaud, Brecht, Joe Hill, Emily Dickinson (and McGrath himself), who desired to confront the future 'on all fours'. None of Dickinson's poetry was published over her name in her lifetime; McGrath's poetry was blacklisted during the Cold War; Brecht's major plays were written in exile, when he had no realistic hope or expectation that they would ever be staged in a German theatre.

Interestingly, this classification overlaps with that of the Scottish poet and novelist William McIllvanney. 'Aristocratic experience for me is the worship of the past, it says the past has defined what the present and the future will be. Bourgeois, middle-class experience I think is the worship of the present; if it had a coat of arms it would be a hand grasping the material, hold what you've got. I think the essence of the dynamic of working-class experience is that it hasn't arrived yet, they're still travelling, therefore they inhabit the dream.'

McGrath's Outlaws and McIllvanney's dreamers are also members of Dickinson's 'Barefoot-Rank', distinguished by their use of 'mean' language (rather than the high or middle style of Aristotle). As McGrath argued, 'the language is there, all you've got to do is to – like the snake, get out of your skin (which is all the cliché and shit language that you've had) and be a born-again snake, or poet, or snake-poet, or whatever... When Sitting Bull needed to write his death song, he just *said* it. Didn't write it, it was *there*.'

This is a hugely important argument, although it is rarely heard these days: that all poetry – all literature – inhabits the common language of everyday living. The greatness of writers like Bunyan, John Clare, Miguel Hernandez, Lewis Grassic Gibbon, Louis Aragon, Ivor Gurney, Nazim Hikmet, Burns, DH Lawrence – 'Outlaws' in more than one sense, often working in real or linguistic exile – has been to have inhabited this argument and sustained it a long way from the centres of cultural power.

Over the last five hundred years, poetry has lost many of its historic functions. Character has fled to the novel, dialogue to the stage, persuasion to advertising and spin, action to cinema, comedy to television. However, the shared, public music of mean language and common experience remains its greatest asset — the power to communicate, universalise and shape a common human identity (what Tom McGrath called the way in which 'language socialises the unknown'). Only in the last few hundred years has poetry been written down. For most of human history most poetry was anonymous, public and shared, passed on and learned and changed and passed on again. Rhythm, metre and rhyme were not only mnemonics, they enabled listeners to be simultaneously the creators of poetry's common music. It is only in mass-literate societies that poetry becomes privatised, a personalised form of individual expression rather a means of public communication. Here is Byron (an aristocrat, of course) looking down his nose at Peasant Poets:

> Heavens! how the vulgar stare! how crowds applaud!
> How ladies read, the Literati laud!
> Ye happy sons of needless trade!
> Swains! quit the plough, resign the useless spade!
> And now no Boor can seek his last abode,
> No common be inclosed, without an ode.
> Oh! since increased refinement deigns to smile
> On Britain's sons, and bless our genial isle,
> Let Poesy go forth, pervade the whole,
> Alike the rustic, and mechanic soul!
> Ye tuneful cobblers! still your snores prolong,
> Compose at once a slipper and a song;
> May Moorland weavers boast Pindaric skill
> And tailors' lays be longer than their bill...

Palgrave's *Golden Treasury* may have been aimed at the newly-literate readers of 'Labour' and 'Poverty' but it was dedicated to another aristocrat – Tennyson. And anyway, within a generation English poetry had withdrawn up Mount Parnassus altogether, first in the name of Art for Art's Sake, then of Modernism (led by a poet who never lost the American tourist's fascination with the English aristocracy).

Nevertheless, the idea that poetry is a publicly-owned, shared and common language persists at a subterranean level within British culture. For example, poetry plays a significant role in prison life. It is a form of release in an emotionally-strained environment, a means of clarification and self-justification and a kind of public confessional. Poems are learned by heart, copied, passed around and sent out in letters to wives and girlfriends. Poetry and poets (like prisoners who can draw) enjoy a special status inside. It's even a form of currency (especially around Valentine's Day and Mother's

Day). But not many post-New Gen poems lend themselves to being copied and sent out in letters. Their provenance is far too specific, the individual 'voice' too highly individuated, distinctive, personalised. Inmates at the prison where I work don't know what to 'do' with most contemporary poetry. They want poetry, not poets.

Until recently I edited a long-running weekly column of readers' poems in the local evening paper. There I frequently received indignant letters from readers claiming that they were the real authors of poems which had appeared in the paper. It wasn't that they were plagiarists or mistaken or mad, but that – like the inmate at Wormwood Scrubs who once tried to persuade Ken Smith that he had written 'The Wind Hover' – their relationship to a poem they had once read, learned and internalised involved a degree of ownership which made them more than simply consumers. I once published a little poem sent in by a reader about a shepherd. It was an unremarkable poem, only dignified by the line 'His drowsy flock dreams on before him'; although I later discovered that it was in fact part of Walter de la Mare's 'Nod', the original has the much less interesting 'His drowsy flock *streams* on before him'. As the great Scottish poet and folk-song collector Hamish Henderson once said, 'no one can say for sure where MacAlias ends and Anon begins.'

At the beginning of the Second World War, the composer Erik Chisholm set to music a poem by Randall Swingler called 'Sixty Cubic Feet' for performance by Unity Theatre in underground shelters during the Blitz. When the poet Arnold Rattenbury, hearing it sung in the Army, claimed he knew its author, he was told in no uncertain terms that it was an old Durham miners' ballad. The story delighted Swingler, who believed that 'the artist is not a special sort of being, inhabiting a rarefied atmosphere beyond the exigencies of common life. Rather it lies in his essence to have more than usual in common with the generality of men.' 'There are,' he argued, 'too many adept practitioners of language, expert in "the organisation of experience." But unhappily so few of them are alive to anything more than their own individual interests and closely circumscribed emotions that their work, fascinating as it may be to the leisured connoisseur of technical facility, will always be ineffective as a life-force in the development of man in society'. Or as Swingler's friend Tom McGrath put it:

> After the first night, the queen says to the king: 'That was *sooper*! What is it called?' 'Fucking,' says the king. Then, after a moment of aristocratic 'thinking', the queen asks: 'Do the lower classes do it?' 'Yes,' says the king. More 'thinking.' 'Much too good for them!' says queenie.

— *London Magazine,* December 2002/January 2003

REVIEW OF TOM PAULIN, *THE INVASION HANDBOOK*

Who else but Tom Paulin could have embarked on a three-volume study in verse of European history from the end of the First World War to the end of the Second? His celebrity, his polemical interest in politics and history, his intellectual and cultural range, his delight in controversy and the Audenesque manner of his early work (not to mention the support of a £75k grant from NESTA) all seem to suggest that Paulin is uniquely well qualified to carry off such an ambitious project.

Fans of Paulin will find much in *The Invasion Handbook* (Faber) to enjoy. It moves swiftly through a series of splendid cameos from the Treaty of Versailles to the Battle of Britain – Mussolini at Locarno, Lenin in his coffin, Trotsky in Mexico, Michael Koltzov in Prague, Churchill in Downing Street. Written in the thin, flat, uneven Skeltonic two/three beat line Paulin has used since *Liberty Tree*, the pages of *The Invasion Handbook* are thickened with the usual internal rhymes, Irish colloquialisms ('pobby', 'drecky', 'lunk') and some inspired neoligisms ('sarntmajor', 'a boyish almostsimper', 'dulce days', the 'plockplock of horseshoes').

However, Paulin fans will also recognise the voice of impressionist Alistair McGowan in these pages. Parts of *The Invasion Handbook* could have been written by McGowan's *Late Show* caricature, the dazzling dinner-party guest who finds in all Victoria Beckham's conversational gambits a reason to quote Joyce and Yeats. For example, driving through Eskra in Co Tyrone makes Paulin think of *Iskra* and so to the Soviet Union, Stalin's Purges and a suitable quotation from Kant. Writing about the invasion of Norway, the Swedish town of Gällivare reminds Paulin of the word Gulliver, which leads him to suggest that in 1940 Churchill was lost among the Lilliputians. This is Paulin's take on Tyneside in the Depression:

maybe it was also Bede's swallow
– no his sparrow –
gave a flick to the myth
that echoes in the name *Jarrow*?
but the real rhyme
– that is the pith
the bony marrow
in this call it cultural primer
was with *harrow*
that dragged with it *hunger* and *hell*
joined to the juddering *j* of *justice*

This kind of irritating critical tick tells us nothing about unemployment in the North-east in the 1930s. It is the intellectual equivalent of a Hovis advert. The reasons why the Jarrow March has entered myth (rather than any of the six, much bigger, marches organised by the Communist-led NUWM) are political, rather than linguistic. If, after writing 'Bede's swallow' Paulin realised his mistake, why leave it in? There is a good deal of this kind of fussy, tremulous re-writing in the book ('that enormous that super / state', 'a cold night a darksome / night', 'the ragged no the raging spirit', 'their ME108 – or was it a 109/ yes a 109'). What seems at first like carelessness soon becomes simply puzzling. What is gained by breaking words at the end of a line ('mar- / gin', 'Trudj- / man', 'lank- / y', 'mo- / ment')? It is never clear why some parts of the book are in prose. Or why the margins are sprinkled with unattributed quotations, or what their relationship is to the poems which they frame.

Paulin covers himself by calling the book a 'looseleaf epic', like a Schwitters' collage, full of quotations, German, French and Latin, 'orts and scraps torn stamps bits of debris / staled by other men and women / more random than the nicks on a tallystick'. But though he asks, 'in what happens to happen/ who or what makes the mistakes?', his 'looseleaf' method allows him to avoid answering his own question.

Considering that so many British poets in the period about which he is writing *did* try to suggest narrative myths for their times – *The Wasteland*, 'Letter to Lord Byron', *Calamiterror*,

'Farewell Chorus', *The Magnetic Mountain* – Paulin's idea of History as a 'scribble' on an unfinished architectural drawing seems unnecessarily and uncharacteristically coy.

In the absence of a teleology of his own, Paulin falls back on the Myth of Failure ('worse and worse the headlines'). And there is plenty of finger-wagging at failure here. From 'in no way clement' Clemenceau to George Bernard Shaw (damned here because he was not on the German's wanted list in the event of an invasion), *The Invasion Handbook* is never short on incrimination. Paulin's 'poem' about the Italian invasion of Abyssinia consists of a single line from a letter by Evelyn Waugh ('I hope the organmen gas them to buggery / love evelyn'). A page of quotations by BUF member Henry Williamson is decorated with a stamp from the Bodelian Library and a daring reminder that Williamson was published by Paulin's own publisher Faber and Faber.

The Invasion Handbook works on such a level of historical allusion, echo and half-quotation (from Eliot, Yeats and Donne to Cornford, Milton and Sterne) that few readers are going to catch all the references (the only individuals who are given historical footnotes are Briande, Stresemann and Austen Chamberlain). On the other hand, to reference it properly would be to make much of the book redundant. If the phrase 'Danish thatch' in 'The Emigration of the Poets' (reprinted here from *The Windog*) makes readers look at Brecht's Svendborg poems, they are hardy likely to turn back to Tom Paulin to learn more about the experience of German exiles after 1933. Addressing the genuine heroism and undeniable barbarism of the Second World War is likely to prove rather harder than writing about pre-war diplomacy, not least because anything Paulin writes about, say, Anzio, El Alamein or the Arctic Convoys is going to have to bear comparison with the heroic poetry written at the time by those who were there.

And this is the central weakness of the whole enterprise, which Paulin needs to address if the next two volumes are going to be anything more than Jackdaw-packs of his own reading. For example, the Spanish Civil War is 'covered' by a prose account of Orwell in Barcelona:

> Eileen got papers and passports ready. She distributed the money she was holding for various ILP members who were still at large, and met the three in the station at the last possible moment before the train left for France. Incredibly, the train has left early. So they hid out a third night and then made for the station again. They smiled and spoke cheerfully and confidently like happy tourists or delegates returning from a lively conference.

Compare Bernard Crick's life of Orwell:

> Eileen, having got papers and passports together, and paid back personal money she was holding fort various ILP members still at large, met them at the station at the last possible moment before the evening train left for France – which they then found, incredibly for Spain, had left early. So a third night was spent hiding out before the four of then got on the morning train together and sat confidently in the restaurant car, as if they were tourists or delegates returning from some conference.

Much of *The Invasion Handbook* is like this, second-rate, third-hand history, the 1930s reduced to extracts from an undergraduate reading-list. Too many historical events are mediated here by the presence of writers Paulin has read – the Treaty of Versailles (Keynes), Locarno (Joyce), the invasion of Abyssinia (Waugh), the German diaspora (Brecht), the betrayal of Czechoslovakia (Gellhorn), the Battle of Britain (Hilary), the fall of Poland (Serallier), the work of SOE (Szabo), life in Nazi Germany (Klemperer).

This is how they used to do history, Carlyle's 'the history of the world is but the biography of great men'. To be fair, Paulin is good at the big decisions taken at the top table. The best parts of the book are those which take us behind the scenes at Versailles and Locarno. No doubt Paulin is already looking forward to writing about Teheran and Potsdam in the third volume in the series. But a history of Europe reduced to the lives of Chaps with Maps is a curiously depopulated one. Top-down history like this has nothing to say about economics, society, fashion, popular culture or music. Paulin has plenty to say about the big-names of High-Modernism (Schwitters, Benjamin, Joyce, the Bauhaus), but nothing about, say, the impact of jazz and Hollywood on British popular culture in this period. It goes without saying that there are hardly any women in the book. The British people are not even a chorus like Auden's 'Mr and Mrs A'. Hooper isn't given a crowd scene until the beaches at Dunkirk.

The Invasion Handbook tells us that European history between the Wars was full of Very Bad Things – the Versailles Treaty, Hitler, TS Eliot, Mussolini's dress-sense, Evelyn Waugh, Lord Halifax, Auden's departure for the USA, Franco, Henry Williamson, Ukrainian nationalism, Albert Speer, Lenin, Stalin (but not Trotsky) and a few Very Good Things (the Locarno Pact, the POUM, James Joyce, the Jarrow March). The history of the Weimar Republic is conjured with a series of apparently random banalities ('The occupation of the Rhineland led to galloping inflation', 'Cross-dressing became very popular', 'Everything on the sexual front was permitted', 'Hitler at high society banquets didn't know how to eat artichoke'). Paulin is hardly more original about Franco's Spain ('By idealising the customs, religion, folklore of Spain before it became an industrialized country, those Spaniards who supported Franco sought to turn their pride into a political ideology... A society built on the preservation of such attitudes is a type of fossil, an empty form which lacks any vital principle.') Describing Stalin as looking like a 'maitre d'hotel' may be effective in a snooty sort of way, but it won't do to use exactly the same comparison for Mussolini. Lord Halifax's comparison of Goering to a 'head gamekeeper' may tell us something about both men, but calling Hitler 'a pied piper' and Lenin a 'Frankenstein's monster' tells us nothing at all. Ribbentrop may have been a 'former champagne salesman', but why refer to Churchill as 'that former naval person'?

We are shown the Jarrow March, but not the General Strike; Chamberlain and Daladier after Munich, but not Willie Gallacher (who made the only speech in the Commons denouncing the Munich agreement); London in the Black-out, but not the storming of the Underground by Londoners during the Blitz; Stalin's purges, but not the Popular Front; the death of George V, but not the death of Valentino; the *Times* but not the (much more pro-Hitler) *Daily Mail*; upper-class appeasers but not middle-class admirers of Hitler or working-class followers of Stalin. There are no contradictions here except the historical ironies afforded by what we now know (a red sunset over Berchtesgaden, for example, is of course a 'cloak of blood'). *The Invasion Handbook* offers little sense that events could have been different, no sense of agency or choice, just the smug judgements of hindsight. 'I never knew the name Auschwitz' declares the idealistic Austen Chamberlain. And a poem about Eliot is entitled – in case we didn't understand the consequences of anti-Semitism – 'The Yellow Spot:

> – then not to embarrass
> each other they play a favourite game
> and try to come up – yes come up –
> with a rhyme for Ritz
> no not Biarritz
> murmurs Tom if we test our wits
> there must be some place some name
> far away to the east
> – maybe you can tell me what fits?

Of course we can, for the same reasons that Eliot couldn't. The question for historians – and poets – born later is not what 'fits' but *why*. Why was there such a close fit between Modernism and Fascism? What is the proper fit between literature and politics? Eliot's dinner-table game is hardly any less tasteless than the one which Tom Paulin seems to be playing throughout *The Invasion Handbook*.

— *London Magazine,* October/November 2003

POETS STAND AGAINST WAR

When the Communist Chilean poet Pablo Neruda was forced to go into hiding in 1948, he once risked taking a late-night taxi across Santiago. Afraid that the driver might betray him to the police, Neruda sat in the shadows in the back of the cab. When they pulled up outside a safe house, he tried to pay the driver. Without looking at Neruda the man replied, 'You don't owe me a thing, Don Pablo. Good luck.'

There are not many British poets who have ever inspired this kind of popular feeling. Few people would recognise the faces of most contemporary British poets, never mind their work.

But something is changing. The Blair-Bush wars are beginning to wake up poets to the world they inhabit. Even the Poet Laureate, Andrew Motion, has written against the invasion of Iraq. Among the surprise best-sellers of the last twelve months were *Authors take Sides on Iraq,100 Poets Against the War* and *Red Sky at Night: an Anthology of British Socialist Poetry*. Elsewhere there was *Poètes Contre La Guerre* (France), *Poetry Against War* (the USA), *Irish Writers Against War* (Ireland) and *100 Gedichte Gegen den Krieg* (Germany).

This week sees some of the best-known poets in the UK joining together as 'Poets for Peace' at the Conway Hall in London to raise money for medical supplies for children in Iraq. The reading is part of Stop the War Coalition's '7 Days for Iraq', a week of events across the country leading up to Armistice Day.

On Monday there is a classical music concert at Hackney Town Hall given by the Medici Quartet, the Moscow Piano Trio and featuring the world premiere of Jordanian composer M.I. Qhandour's *Cry Jerusalem.*

On Tuesday evening (US election night) there will be a reading in Trafalgar Square of the names of the 25,000 killed since the invasion of Iraq in March 2003. Readers include Ken Livingstone, Stephen Hawking, Harold Pinter, Rose Gentle, Neil Pearson, Juliet

Stevenson, Suzie Orbach, Jeremy Corbyn MP, Kate Hudson and Peter Kennard.

'Poets for Peace' features some of Britain's best-known writers and performers – Brian Patten, Shadow Poet Laureate Adrian Mitchell and Jean Binta Breeze. Chrstopher Logue is reading from his translations of Homer, ex-Python Terry Jones will be reading some of his satiric stories about President Bush and Jonathan Pryce, fresh from his role in the West End hit *The Goat*, is reading translations of contemporary Iraqi poets

'Poets for Peace' are united by friendship, opposition to the Blair-Bush wars and a belief that poetry can make a difference. 'There will be poems about the war,' says organiser Celia Mitchell, 'though this is not agitprop but a life-affirming and enjoyable reading to help us through these terrible times.'

For some readers Brian Patten will be a surprising recruit to the anti-war cause. He is, after all, better known as a poet of love than of war. But Patten is impatient of those who say that poets should keep clear of politics ('breathing is political!') 'The more poetry can touch people,' he says, 'the more you can raise people's awareness, help them to think, "hang on, we can do something too".' 'All war is one war,' he says, quoting Christopher Logue, 'All wars are civil wars.' 'Poetry *can* make things happen,' he argues. Brian will be reading some new poems on Thursday including his recent verse adaptations of Sufi stories.

Adrian Mitchell will be reading from his new collection *The Shadow Knows*, which he dedicated to the Peace Movement. 'Poetry is about creativity, about birth and babies and life,' he says, 'poetry is to do with peace, not to do with killing and war. Unfortunately, because wars go on and on and on poets still have to write about war.'

Thanks to Mitchell, there will be a special guest appearance by William Blake, with Jonathan Pryce performing extracts from the Adrian Mitchell/Mike Westbrook show *Tyger*:

Let the slave grinding at the mill run out into the
        field
Let him look up into the heavens & laugh in the
        bright air
Let the unchained soul, shut up in darkness and in
        sighing
Whose face has never seen a smile in thirty weary
        years
Rise up and look out; his chains are loose, his
        dungeon doors are open;
And let his wife and children return from the
        oppressor's scourge
They look behind at every step & believe it is a dream
Singing: The Sun has left his blackness & has found a
        fresher morning
And the fair Moon rejoices in the clear & cloudless
        night
For empire is no more and now the Lion & the Wolf
        shall cease.
For everything that lives is Holy.

Perhaps on Friday morning a London cabbie will say, 'I had that William Blake in my cab last night. Or was it that Brian Patten?'

— *Morning Star*, 2 November 2004

THE DARK ART OF POETRY

In his TS Eliot lecture at the Royal Festival Hall's Poetry International, Don Paterson recently called for poetry to reclaim its status as 'a Dark Art'. Poetic technique, he declared, is 'the poet's arcana', 'something that must be kept secret from the reader'. Only by joining together in a kind of medieval 'guild', could professional poets 'restore our sense of power'. Cue scary laughter.

It was splendidly dotty stuff, part Gilderoy Lockhart, part Draco Malfoy, well-timed for Halloween and the DVD release of the new Harry Potter. But if poets are to belong to a 'guild', a kind of elite, secret society of magicians (something like Slytherin, perhaps) who are the Muggles?

Paterson was quite clear about this, calling for the 'total eradication of amateur poets', whom he accuses of 'infantilising poetry'. Worse, armed only with 'a beermat, a pencil, and a recently mildly traumatic experience' they bombard Don Paterson, who is poetry editor at Picador, with their 'handwritten drivel'.

But professional poets do not spring fully armed from the soil. You have to be unpublished before you can be published. It may be hard to imagine, but even Don Paterson was once an unpublished poet. Not many poets make a living solely by selling books. Don Paterson (who has received three Scottish Arts Council Book Awards) certainly doesn't. Before he became a 'professional' poet, he used to be a professional musician. He still is. In fact, he is also a lecturer at the University of St Andrews. Not much time for writing poetry there.

Anyway, what is an 'amateur' poet? For most of human history poetry was mostly anonymous, unwritten. public and shared. It is only with the recent emergence of mass-literate societies in the West that it has become identified with the private expression of individual feeling in books by 'professional' poets.

Does Paterson (whose most recent book won the Whitbread Prize) mean he wants to eradicate unpublished poets? Or just those who have ambitions to be published? Those who are not published by a London publisher? Or those who are not published by Picador? How many poetry-prizes do you have to win before you become 'professional' poet? Or is there a hereditary principle involved?

Paterson's idea of the 'profession' of poetry seems to derive from a class-specific version of the Sorting Hat at Hogwarts. According to Paterson (winner of the Geoffrey Faber Memorial Award) 'only plumbers can plumb, roofers can roof and drummers drum; only poets can write poetry.' Has Paterson never changed a tap, or tapped a drum? Poets are not genetically different from plumbers. Most roofers will be better at writing poetry than poets are at replacing missing roof-tiles. Paterson seems to be invoking the old Soviet model in which you had to be a member of the Writers Union before you could be published.

It is not as if there are only so many as-yet-unwritten poems to go round. Moreover, 'amateur' poets in schools, colleges, prisons, libraries, book-shops and poetry-readings constitute the bulk of the audience for the 'professionals'. Do professional musicians feel threatened by people who sing in the bath? Do professional footballers burn with resentment at those who play in Sunday leagues? Do professional chefs object to the thought that most people cook their own meals? Presumably Paterson's students at St Andrews are 'amateurs'. Has he told them they require 'eradicating' yet?

Patterson's comments on Harold Pinter are especially instructive. Referring to Pinter's anti-war poetry, he says that '*anyone* can do that'. Of course, a great many poets – 'professional' and 'amateur' – have written powerfully against the invasion of Iraq (although few have employed iambic pentameter to such passionate effect as Pinter did in *War*). The fact that 'anyone' can write about such a necessary subject, is precisely the enduring appeal and significance of poetry.

Unfortunately, hostility to the idea of the amateur is a familiar feature of the contemporary poetry scene. The sound of 'professional' poets pulling the ladders up behind them is part of the background noise. The more that people write poetry, the more some poets squeal about the dilution of their 'profession'. The Poetry Society may spend its time declaring that poetry belongs to everyone, sponsoring initiatives like National Poetry Day, Poetry Class and *Poetry News*, but it also publishes the forbidding and mysterious *Poetry Review,* a magazine apparently designed to put any casual reader off poetry for good.

The most consistent advocate of this kind of flaky elitism was TS Eliot, the Lord Voldemort of the aristocratic principle in poetry. Fittingly Don Paterson (the only poet to win the TS Eliot Prize twice) made his remarks in a lecture named after a man who believed in the Divine Right of kings and who argued that the 1944 Education Act would encourage cultural 'barbarism'.

But this is a small crack on a wider fault-line in British literary culture – and in British society. Don Paterson (winner of the Forward Prize) was tapping into a peculiarly English use of the word 'amateur' as a term of abuse. Like 'provincial', 'humorous' and 'earnest', it involves a horrified rejection of the aspirational rhetoric of New Labour Britain. And it smells uncommonly like old-fashioned snobbery and misanthropy.

As Hagrid says, 'when a wizard goes over ter the Dark Side, there's nothin' and no one that matters to 'em anymore.' Scary.

— *New Statesman,* 6 December 2004

EXCLUDED

In 2003 BBC Radio Four made a documentary about a week writing poetry with students at an EBD School in Spennymoor, Co Durham. Produced by Caroline Beck, 'Excluded' was first broadcast on 13 March 2003.

Going into schools these days is a complicated business. You are expected to be entertaining *and* funny *and* accessible. You are often there so that the school can show it has taken steps to address literacy problems identified in the last OFSTED report, and to help the school promote itself in the local paper. You are required to help deliver the national literacy strategy, and more often than not to address issues like bullying, drugs and racism. You are supposed to help raise levels of self-esteem, especially among working-class children. You are expected to inspire reluctant male readers to pick up a book and enjoy it. You are somehow supposed to legitimise the world of books. And if all that were not enough, these days poetry must do its bit to tackle issues of social exclusion.

It's an impossible task, of course. Not least because poets and poetry have done so much to make people feel that they are excluded from the world of literature, creativity and poetry, that they do not belong, that most books are written by and for and about other kinds of people. 'Exclusion' is not only an economic description; it's a cultural one too. It's all very well to assert that poetry belongs to everyone. But that's not how it feels to most people. Why should children in am EBD school like The Meadows be expected to take any interest in poetry? What's in it for them?

These 'reluctant male readers' (such a delicate euphemism, as though reading is the only thing they are reluctant to do) can be a scary lot. I try to armour myself with the books I have written, mostly about football, for Hodder/Livewire. Football may be an easy button to press, but it rarely fails to arouse some interest among the boys on the back row who at first don't see the books, only their subjects. Occasionally this can rebound – if they do not like a particular player or team, they will not like a book about them, still less respect a writer who could write a book about them.

But these books help to establish my credentials, first as a writer ('Are you famous then?'), second as someone who thinks and feels like they do ('Who do you support then ?') and third *as a writer who thinks and feels like they do* ('You don't look like a writer!') When asked what they thought a poet would look like, all the kids in the Meadows School said they thought I would wear a suit; one thought I would wear a cravat and talk posh. 'But he's not like that,' said another – 'he's got a face and everything!'

It is difficult to over-state the size of the cultural and psychological barriers that stand between so many children and the world of books. It is also easy to under-estimate how little most children understand about the way a book is made (I am often asked if I draw the pictures in my football books – which are of course photographs). My books about, say, David Beckham, Alan Shearer or Michael Owen, 'naturalise' the world of reading and writing in ways that none of my other books – poetry, literary criticism and biography – ever could.

But books themselves are not enough to inspire reluctant readers to read. They won't become readers until they have become writers. They won't read if they won't write. They won't write if they think writing belongs to someone else. They won't respect, or be curious about, or be passionate about, or be critical of, other people's writing until they begin to be some of those things about their own writing. Books won't belong in their lives until their lives belong in books.

In my experience the quickest and most effective way of turning reluctant readers into writers is through poetry. The self-conscious use of heightened, patterned, musical language can encourage a sense of the magic of words, a feeling for the unsuspected power and pleasure of using language with care and economy and precision, and an understanding of the importance of memory and anticipation. Half an hour of improvised, rhythmical, rhyming, whole-class poems (not necessarily even written down) which 'funnel' everyone towards the missing rhymes, can quickly encourage a sense of ownership over poetry.

You don't have to be 'good at English' to write poetry. Poetry is both familiar and unfamiliar, both recognisably strange and strangely recognisable, a democratic creative act that is both equally hard and equally easy for everyone, whether you are a reader or not. Ask most children to write a story and the results will be unremarkable. Even the kids who are 'good at English' will write the way they talk, as they talk the way they think. And it won't feel or look much like the kind of story that ends up in a book. But poetry has special rules – rhythm, rhyme, echo, alliteration, stanza-shape, diction etc – which won't let you reach for the first word that comes into your head. You can't write the way you talk. You have to attend to the rules of the game. Your words have to fit the pattern. You have to become a writer. And even the most tentative, second-hand poem looks like a 'real' poem once it is typed up, stuck on the wall, turned into an A3 poster, published in a school-magazine or local newspaper. Once you have become a writer, then just possibly you might become a reader.

Instead of asking the children at The Meadows to write poems in English lessons, we decided to take poetry across the entire syllabus. So we wrote geometric poems in Maths, poems about electricity and magnets in Science, poems about shopping in Geography. Last lesson each day a dedicated group of editors sat and typed up all the poems written during the day. By Friday afternoon we had produced a 32-page, stapled booklet, *Rhyming Riddles and Dizzy Diddles* including valentines acrostics, alliterative poems, a Macbeth rap, a blessing for a new-born baby, poems about numbers, poems about pets, and poems about kissing. Everyone in the school was given a copy. Almost all the children in the school saw their name in print for the first time.

It was hard work, and the results weren't always very edifying. There were some bad moments that week – the boy who escaped by climbing between the bars at the window, the fight in the dining-room, the deputy head punched in the face, the boy who spent several hours in a police cell.

But there were some utterly memorable moments too. Late one morning, shortly before dinner-time, when all the boys in the room seemed to be asleep, a bird flew in through the window into the classroom. There was pandemonium. Suddenly everyone was wide awake, running across the desks, trying to catch the bird. Other kids ran in to see what the noise was about. Then, just as suddenly, one of the boys stood still in the middle of the room, as if in a trance, and began improvising, out loud, a poem about what was happening. The whole room went quiet. It was as though he was speaking in tongues. Having being exposed to the language and the music of poetry for two days, Darren had found within him the primitive, magical origins of all art – in collective experience, in the real or ritual taming of nature, and in Orphic utterance. And although he may not have been conscious of it, at some level Darren understood that the bird was a metaphor for the creativity that was struggling to break free inside him.

At that moment, however briefly, we were all 'included', not in some tacky New Labour stakeholder-dream of student loans and private health insurance, but in the shared, common humanity that poetry can still reveal:

> I was sat in my lesson
> When a bird flew by
> Out of the sky.
> It came through the window,
> It was trying to get out
> By banging into everything.
> It was just a little blue tit.
> We opened the window more
> And then the radio woman Caroline
> Caught it by putting her hand out
> And grabbing it.
> Then she let it go,
> Very slowly.

— An edited version of this appeared in Mandy Coe and Jean Sprackland (eds) *Our Thoughts are Bees: Writers Working with Schools* (Wordplay Press, 2005)

ADRIAN MITCHELL 1932-2008

Sometime in 1968, Adrian Mitchell addressed a Youth CND demonstration against the US war on Vietnam. Among the crowd was the usual Special Branch plod, who solemnly wrote in his report that 'Adrian Mitchell recited one of his poems, the meaning of which was largely unintelligible...'

Mitchell believed that British secret services had been interested in him ever since, as a student he attended a Communist Party wine and cheese event 'for peace'. 'I wasn't a Communist,' he said, 'but I like wine. And cheese. And peace. I hope they still have their notebooks open, because I'm still doing this stuff.'

When the Home Office were asked, under the Freedom of Information Act, to release their files on Mitchell, they said that they could 'neither confirm nor deny' their existence, since to do so might threaten 'national security'.

It's a ludicrous though instructive story, which says much about British political culture. On one hand there is something called the 'national' interest, defined by people for whom poetry is 'largely unintelligible'. On the other hand – food, wine, peace and poetry. But it is good to know that at least someone considers Adrian Mitchell's life and work as being of national importance.

Adrian Mitchell was far too radical a writer to become a 'national treasure'. But he was undoubtedly a national figure, a widely respected poet, novelist, playwright, librettist and children's writer, and a uniquely popular performer who took his poetry to schools and festivals and readings all over the world for more than fifty years.

He was the only British poet invited to the inauguration of Thabo Mbeki as South African President 1999. In 2005 his poem 'Human Beings' was voted the poem that people would most like to send into space as a message from Earth. His famous lines, 'Most people ignore most poetry because most poetry ignores most people' have recently been reproduced on a T-shirt from Philosophy Football.

Adrian Mitchell enjoyed the most glittering of writing careers. And yet it was curiously free of the usual glittering prizes. He received an Eric Gregory Award in 1961, a PEN Translation Prize in 1966 for *Marat/Sade* and a PBS Best Children's Collection in 2004 for *Daft as a Doughnut*. And that's it. It's a poor reflection on British life. But perhaps honouring our greatest poet while he was alive would have threatened 'national security'.

Of course, Mitchell would have been the first to dismiss the shabby world of literary prize-giving. After all, he liked to describe himself as 'a socialist-anarchist-pacifist-Blakeist-revolutionary'. As the broadsheets and the bookies contemplate the choice of the next poet laureate, it is worth remembering Adrian Mitchell's description of the work of the laureate, 'as this: / A long, thin streak of yellow piss.' He once said he would only consider the job only if he was allowed to 'tap-dance on the coffin at every Royal Funeral'. Asked once by the *Telegraph* to write a poem about Prince Charles he responded with, 'Royalty is a neurosis. Get well soon.'

British literary life usually knows how to separate radical writers from their politics, which are conventionally 'explained' or subsumed by other identities – Sylvia Townsend-Warner was gay, Day Lewis was never really comfortable with politics, John Cornford was looking for martyrdom, Edgell Rickword was silenced by orthodoxy, Patrick Hamilton was a drunk etc. But it is clearly impossible to separate Adrian Mitchell's personality from his work or from his politics. He really was as kind and generous and radical in his life as he was in his poetry. A great poet as well as a great bloke. You can't have one without the other.

Because Adrian Mitchell was so good on stage, it is perhaps easy to forget how good a poet he was on the page. As though his poetry lived in the shadow of its author. And of course he was the most wonderful of readers, whose distinctive manner of performing his work was like a kind of syncopated dance, part prayer, part giggle. Orpheus *and* Dionysus, Lennon and McCartney, Ginsberg and Guthrie.

He was the wisest and most eloquent of the Children of Albion, William Brown meets William Blake, mischievous and 'innocent' like the boy who is not afraid to ask why the Emperor is not wearing any clothes. He combined the jazz-poetry of the North American Beats, the radical folk tradition of Latin American communists like Victor Jara, and the Springtime optimism of Soviet troubadours like Yevtushenko and Voznesensky (Kenneth Tynan once called him 'the British Mayakovsky'). He was the inheritor of a peculiarly English tradition of nonsense, nursery and cautionary tales, from Carroll and Lear, Belloc and Chesterton, to Ivor Cutler and Spike Milligan. He wrote with the unflinching seriousness of Brecht (see, for example, his stunning version of 'Von der Kindesmörderin Marie Farrar'). And he was the nearest equivalent in British literary life to the French writer Jacques Prévert, writing playful, punning and apparently childish little fables that packed an extraordinary punch – irreverent, anti-intellectual, unpicking the logic of authority and war.

Adrian Mitchell was a truly great poet. We must not forget this. His Bloodaxe collections, *Heart on the Left: Poems 1953-85, Blue Coffee: Poems l986-l995, All Shook Up: Poems 1996-2000* and *The Shadow Knows: Poems 2000-2004* are an extraordinary and incomparable achievement. He wrote many great and justly famous individual poems, but now they are collected under one roof they may be seen to constitute a single, huge, sprawling epic for our times, comical and visionary, heartening and heart-breaking.

— *The North* no 43, Summer 2009

REVIEW OF FRED VOSS, *HAMMERS AND HEARTS*
OF THE GODS

When was the last time you read a decent book about work? People don't work very much in contemporary literature. The narrow social basis of British literary culture means that work and working-class life is largely limited to the melodrama of TV soaps and the comic caricatures of ASBO-land.

But in the USA, the world of work – especially casual, low-paid, manual work – is still central to myths of selfhood and nationhood. Hollywood constantly celebrates and romanticises working-class masculinity. Writers like Whitman, Melville, Steinbeck, Sinclair and Frost placed work at the heart of the US literary tradition. Today magazines like *Blue Collar Review, Pemmican* and *Left Curve* are committed to publishing blue-collar poetry. There are even several websites dedicated solely to poetry written by long-distance truckers.

For the last thirty years Fred Voss has been working as a machinist in factories in southern California. *Hammers and Hearts of the Gods* (Bloodaxe Books, £8.95) is his third British collection, an extraordinary, moving, funny, complex study of life and work on the factory floor.

Voss writes wonderfully well about fellow machinists, men who are sometimes 'only one step up from County Jail', their frustrations and satisfactions, their hangovers and quiet breakdowns, and the violence, beauty and tenderness of which they are capable ('I have seen men go to every extreme they can / to prove / they are still / human'). These are mostly men

> who cannot afford a pair of glasses a haircut
> shoelaces
> a meal a room... men
> one hair's breadth away
> from suicide
> madness
> prison
> the street

> men
> getting poorer penny by penny each day each year
> without hope
> of a raise.

Yet they are also giants, constantly remaking the world through collective planning, labour and skill. For Voss, poetry can be 'tough as tool steel heat-treated to Rockwell 60 / hardness', or soft as 'the lines / carved into the skin of the old lathe operator's hands'. And it can be found 'in toolboxes / drill size charts / the teeth / of cutters ground sharp as razors on the black diamond wheel'.

The whole book is a sustained hymn to work, its dull rituals and comfortable routines, its winners and losers. It records the exhaustion and boredom, the camaraderie and the loneliness, the bleak and painful weirdness of work. Through work we change the world and thereby change ourselves – 'the one thing the waves / the watches/ the spiders / the spaghetti recipes the acorns and every last thing in this universe was born / to do: / work'.

The fact that his factory makes helicopter parts for the US military gives Voss a chilling but wholly original take on 9/11 and the wars in Afghanistan and Iraq. On the other hand, he reminds himself, Louis Armstrong's trumpet was man-made. So were Roosevelt's aluminium braces, the train that carried Martin Luther King to Washington in 1963 and the coffee machine that sobers up the man so he can 'find his way back into a machine shop / to step up to a machine / that can cut stinking steel smoking in cutting oil down into the shape / of a dream'.

Above all, the collective patterns of the modern industrial process encourage him to see the possibility of organising the world differently –

> as the boss comes down the aisle cold and angry
> and screaming for parts
> I wait
> for the soothing touch of that sun on my fingers to
> tell me
> that someday

we may put our cold competitive time clocks and
bosses away
and find a warmer way
to live.

— *Morning Star,* 7 September 2009

REVIEW OF JAMES BYRNE AND CLARE POLLARD (EDS)
VOICE RECOGNITION: 21 POETS FOR THE 21ST CENTURY
AND RODDY LUMSDEN (ED) *IDENTITY PARADE*

Generational anthologies have always defined themselves as the bearers of the 'new'. *New Signatures, New Country, The New Apocalypse, New Lines* and *The New Poetry* all successfully challenged existing tastes by claiming to represent the future.

It is therefore perhaps inevitable that James Byrne and Clare Pollard (eds) *Voice Recognition: 21 Poets for the 21st Century* (Bloodaxe) should snootily declare war on the 'uncool' poetry of 'warm white wine in a pokey bookshop or plodding recitals in a half empty village hall.'

The book brings together twenty-one 'of the best young poets who have yet to publish a full collection' from Britain and Ireland, who are apparently 'extending and remaking the tradition of poetry in a fast-changing new millennium', whose work is 'sexy', 'dark', 'daring' and 'brimming with vitality'. 'The future of poetry,' claim the editors, 'begins here'.

In many ways it is a fascinating selection, a good sample of some of the poets who have emerged out of the performance-publishing nexus of Generational Txt, Spread the Word, Apples and Snakes, the Foyles Young Poetry of the Year Award, the tall-lighthouse Pilot project and the world of Creative Writing MAs. And there are some genuine new talents here – notably Joe Dunthorne, Amy Blakemore, Siddartha Bose, Jay Bernard and Toby Martinez de las Rivas.

But it is a pretty depressing read too. At best it's a collection of confessional poetry, filmic sensibilities and 'a multiplicity of styles'. Poetry for the Face-Book generation. So there are lots of ampersands, lower-case titles and references to high art and trash-culture. But there is not a single rhyme in the book, not enough anger and hardly any laughs (the one exception is Ahren Warner's great 'About suffering they were never wrong, the old Masters').

And if these poets share 'a deep fascination with the world as it is today', you would hardly not know it from this book which barely mentions the world's social inequalities, the destruction of the environment or the globalised economics of poverty and war – never mind those popular movements trying to make another world possible.

Roddy Lumsden (ed) *Identity Parade* (Bloodaxe) makes more modest claims. It aims not to be 'a canonical document of an era, but to spread the word, to educate and recommend' some of the poets who have emerged since the mid-1990s.

There are eighty-five poets here, including many justly famous names, like Patience Agbabi, Colette Bryce, Bernardine Evaristo, Jen Hadfield, Gwyneth Lewis, Alice Oswald, Deryn Rees-Jones, Neil Rollinson and Jean Sprackland, as well as impressive newcomers like Frances Leviston and Daljit Nagra. And it is good to see so many women poets included – there are in fact more women writers than men.

But although the book hopes to reflect 'the pluralist now', it is unavoidably a partial – even a partisan – selection. Nearly a quarter of these poets have published only a single book; three have not even published one. When there are so many glaring omissions – not just of names, but of places, publishers, subjects, voices, constituencies – the inclusion of so many newcomers narrows the book's claims even further.

There are lots of poetry worlds out there. These two books – useful and enjoyable though they may be – represent just one of them.

— *Morning Star,* 14 April 2010

QU'EST-CE LE COMMUNISME?

For Bertolt Brecht, it was 'the simple idea so hard to achieve.' For Ronald Reagan, it was a 'sad, bizarre chapter in human history'. For Stephen Spender it was the 'God that Failed'. But for the French poet Francis Combes,

> Communism (or whatever you'd prefer to call it) is
> nothing
> but the common future of humanity.
> Its possibilities are written in the present as its
> negation and continuation,
> a seed in the earth, the spring in winter, the child in
> its parents.

These lines are taken from *Cause Commune*, an extraordinary poetic history of the Communist idea, from the Garden of Eden to the fall of the Berlin Wall. It is a huge book in every sense, 200 poems over 300 pages, a brave and original essay on utopianism, revolution and hope. It is a study of the Communist movement in the twentieth-century, the men and women who led it, like Lenin, Luxemburg, Trotsky and Gramsci, as well as some of the artists who marched in its ranks, like Mayakovsky, Picasso and Brecht. It is a history of the defeated, a book about enthusiasm and illusion, heroes and martyrs, saints and sinners. It is an epic, a tragedy and a manifesto for the utopian imagination.

Although the book was ignored by the critics when it was first published in 2003, it is already in its fourth edition. Parts have been translated into German and Arabic. And this month sees the first English translation of *Common Cause* (Smokestack Books) in a translation by Alan Dent, with a foreword by John Berger.

Francis Combes started writing the book just before the fall of the Berlin Wall, working on it over the next twelve years. 'For me, it was a question of taking stock of the situation, of the history of revolution, of the epic poem of communism, its hope and its tragedy. I wanted to show that we don't have to condemn an idea just because it is betrayed. Communism, like Christianity, has had its apostles, its saints, its martyrs, its traitors, its corrupt popes, its inquisitors, its thinkers and its poets. It is an ancient dream, found in every culture, philosophy and religion. That is why, in spite of everything, we cannot give it up.'

He joined the Jeunesse communiste when he was just fourteen. At university – where he studied Politics and Oriental Languages – he was general secretary of the Union of Communist Students (then the largest student organisation in France). Later he was elected as PCF Conseiller général for Val d'Oise. Today, Combes is one of the leaders of the left wing inside the PCF and a founder of the newspaper *Manifesto*. Last year he launched an appeal, signed by a hundred of European intellectuals, to support the idea of a Fifth International – 'faced with the total crisis of capitalism,' he says, 'we need a socialism of the twenty-first century, drawing lessons of the experiments of the last century and capable of taking up the actual challenges of the planet.'

Francis Combes began writing poetry began at a very early age.

> I copied out the poems which my mother, a teacher, taught her pupils. And if I liked them, I signed them with my own name! In a sense, I still think we have to appropriate the poems which we most like. Poetry belongs to everyone. Only by copying can you learn to be original. Of course, as a teenager, I wrote lots of bad love poems. But it was good to get rid of the harmful influence of Baudelaire. It was only after this that I began finding my own voice and my own way. A poet, you might say, is somebody who has never abandoned the mistakes of their youth. Writing poetry is for me a simple necessity. Why? To speak up for those who are silent. To support the right to dream of beauty in a world which no longer dreams of the future. Because I am not perfect, and nor is the world.

To date, Combes has published fifteen books of poetry. He has translated many poets into French, including Heine, Brecht, Mayakovsky and Attila Joszef. He is a founder of the radical publishing cooperative, Le Temps des Cerises (named after a song about the Paris Commune). And for many years he was responsible for putting poems on the Paris Metro.

Asked to name the poets who have most influenced him, he reels off a long list – Villon, Apollinaire, Ronsard, Hugo, Rimbaud, Khlebnikov, Neruda, Ritsos, Whitman, Heine, Ginsberg, Ferlinghetti, Dalton, Cardenal, and Resistance poets like Eluard, Aragon, Marcenac, Gaucheron and Guillevic. 'I probably learn more from reading foreign poets than French poets,' he says, 'because they can enlarge my skyline and my ideas about what poetry can say today on the banks of the Seine.'

Combes is part of the generation of French poets – Gérard Noiret, Guy Goffette, Serge Pey, Yvon le Men, Jean-Pierre Siméon, George Hassomeris and Françoise Coulmin – who emerged in the 1980s, committed to putting lyricism, satire and politics back into French poetry, what he calls 'la poésie transformelle'.

> Poetry does not belong to a small group of specialists. It arises from the everyday use of language. Like language, poetry only exists because we share it. Writing – like singing, painting and cooking – is a form of sharing. For me poetry is like an electrical transformer which converts our feelings and our ideas into energy. It is a way of keeping your feet on the ground without losing sight of the stars. It is at the same time both the world's conscience and its best dreams; it's an intimate language and a public necessity. The issues at stake French poetry today are profoundly political. It is often said that modern French poetry began with Rimbaud's 'Je est un autre.' Today we need to reverse this phrase and say, 'L'Autre est aussi Je' or even 'Je suis tous les autres'.

On the face of it, these are not good times to ask the question, 'what is Communism?' The world seems to have made up its mind that it is a Bad Thing. But Francis Combes is still optimistic. 'Everywhere, the old mole of history keeps on digging, even in Europe – look at what is happening in Greece. No-one can decree the end of the class struggle. History is not over. There are more surprises still to come. And I do not think for my part that humanity is ready to commit suicide.' Or as he puts it in *Common Cause*,

> Communism (or whatever it turns out to be and
> which will bear
> the name you care to give it or no name at all)
> appears where the wealth hoarded by a few pushes
> life
> to the edge of the abyss, as the vital need
> for public wealth, for sharing and solidarity.

— *Morning Star,* 16 June 2010

INTERVIEW WITH JIM SCULLY

In 1973 the American poet Jim Scully won a prestigious Guggenheim Fellowship to travel abroad for twelve months. Excited by the achievements of the Allende government in Chile, he decided to move his young family to Santiago. They were in Mexico, on their way to Chile, when the army overthrew the government and murdered Allende.

'We went on to Chile anyway, figuring the military would assume I was a US agent. Which they did. Access to the Pudahuel airport was restricted to soldiers and DINA, the intelligence police, mostly guys in business suits carrying automatic weapons. They didn't even check our bags. We were North Americans, our kids were blonde, we were arriving on the heels of the *golpe* – who else could we be but who we had to be?'

Although Jim and his wife Arlene had been involved in the anti-war movement in New Jersey in the early 1960s, living in Chile in the aftermath of the US-backed Pinochet coup was a brutal introduction to political realities. 'Imagine witnessing a woman from the Israeli consulate negotiating a shipment of Uzis with a colonel of the carabineros, at a party with one of the Chicago Boys present.'

One of their neighbours was Isabel Letelier, then living under house arrest. Her husband, who had been Allende's Defence Minister, was later murdered by a car bomb in Washington. For a while, the Scullys' Santiago apartment was used as a safe house by the MIR (*Movimiento de Izquierda Revolucionaria*) guerrillas. 'They'd borrowed a book of my poems (*Avenue of the Americas*), returning it with the verdict: "a little bit hippy, a little Trotskyite, but (pause) very definitely Left." And smiled. Among all else, they had a certain innocence. As did we. No reality is contained by its stereotype.'

Scully returned to the US with his *Santiago Poems*. Sandy Taylor created the now legendary Curbstone Press in order to publish it, 'Behind a TV screen / as in a shadow play / the general gavels his fist. / His captive audience / is 10 million souls... When he opens his mouth / all Santiago / contracts to a shrunken head'.

The Scullys joined the Progressive Labour Party ('lots of street action for five years with some wonderful people, mostly Puerto Rican'). Later, Scully and Taylor were arrested on weapons charges related to anti-KKK activity. In the late 1970s Scully and Taylor published *Art on the Line*, a series of Curbstone booklets by Roque Dalton, Cesar Vallejo, George Grosz, John Heartfield and Wieland Herzfelde.

It was a brave attempt to inform, and raise a few caveats with, mainstream US poetry. But the mainstream, of course, wasn't listening:

> The mainstream does not critically engage work outside its realm. How could it? It can't critically engage itself. The poetic field is no less a political construct than an aesthetic one. When we speak of mainstream poetry, we're talking basically about academic poetry, poetry in its institutional aspect, which is the basis for jobs, careers, publications and poetic norms. It's where the continuity of money and recognition is maintained. There's a lot of cute, too-clever-by-half poetry without an ounce of gravity, and of course no resonance. It seems we lack even the language with which to speak social or civic reality.

Finding that his poetry was unpublishable in US magazines, Scully gave up writing poetry altogether for many years. He began to write critical essays (*Line Break: Poetry as Social Practice*).

> But when the Bush regime broke out its readymade War on Terror immediately after 9/11, I began writing poetry again. By that time the postmodernist thing was incapable of landing hard enough to say anything about anything. Worse, it had extended the tenure of social silence, leaving an opening only for identity politics and the academic discipline called post-colonialism – this with nearly a thousand US military bases, some the size of small cities, installed across the world.

In the last decade Scully has been writing furiously, as though to make up for lost time. He has recently published three collections of poetry, a travel book about the break-up of Yugoslavia and a new translation (with Bob Bagg) of Sophocles' plays. This month sees the publication of *Angel in Flames*, a collection of the best of his poems and translations from the last forty years. It's an extraordinary achievement by any standards, an eloquent and stubborn witness to the victory march of imperialism –

> so Agamemnon lords it still,
> Menelaos struts and struts,
> they can't stop
> lording and strutting...
> and when the gods are gone
> into the long, drunken night –
> gods of the globe
> drunk with blood, drunk with money,
> with hatred of life
> we will go after them
> into the same night.

He points out that in ancient Greece, 'apolitical' citizens, who cared only for their own personal interests, were called *idiotai*:

> This is the opposite of *politai*, citizens in the true sense. For the Greek tragedians, the primary point of collective reference was society, not the individual. They took everything on, and in front of everyone. Full-bodied, adult stuff. Not crimped by the servility that comes of habitual evasiveness.

Among the classical poets Scully most admires is the sixth-century BCE soldier-poet Archilochos, who is supposed to have said that 'the fox knows many things; the hedgehog one big thing.' For Scully, the one big thing is the belief that 'poetry is a struggle for breath'.

> We write poems not because we want to but because we have to. I feel the necessity of speaking to where the social silence is. I'd prefer to be writing other things, but conscience gets me and won't let go.

— *Morning Star,* 11 October 2011

TWENTY-FIRST CENTURY POETRY

This month's column is a bit later than usual because I have been away, reading in Paris. I was there to take part in the long-running International Poetry Biennale in Val-de-Marne (the only Department in the capital still governed by the PCF).

The presiding genius of the festival is the poet Francis Combes. Responsible for many years for putting poems on the Paris Metro, Combes also runs the radical publishing house Le Temps des Cerises. The aim of the festival is to democratise the writing and reading of poetry.

This year's poets included Valerio Magrelli and Maria Grazia Calandrone (Italy), Florence Pazzottu and Gerard Mordillat (France) and Yourgos Markopoulos, Dino Siotis and Thanasis Triaridis (Greece). Between them, these poets are trying to address the crises in contemporary Europe with a passionate eloquence, bitter wisdom and scathing irony.

How depressing then, to arrive back in the UK just in time for the announcement of this year's TS Eliot Prize shortlist. Yes, it's that time of year again when anyone interested in poetry – writers and readers, publishers and critics – is gripped by the overwhelming question: does anyone really give a toss about who wins this year's Prize?

It's the usual carve-up between a small group of publishers – Picador (3), Faber (2), Jonathan Cape (2), Carcanet (2) and Seren (1). And it's the usual dull Poetry Book Society narrative of 'major names' and 'newcomers', bookie's favourites, outsiders and dark-horses.

The fact that there are some excellent writers on this year's list – Deryn Rees-Jones, Simon Armitage and Kathleen Jamie – cannot disguise the intellectual narrowness of the whole enterprise. Two of this year's judges are previous winners of the prize; five of the short-listed authors have been short-listed before; four have judged the prize in previous years. Six titles were chosen by the judges, the other four were PBS quarterly choices (themselves selected by the authors of previous PBS choices).

It's a ludicrous and unpleasant racket. But at least there is no public money involved any more. Having lost its Arts Council support, the PBS is now sponsored by an international investment management firm. Appropriate perhaps, for a literary prize named for a banker, anti-Semite, admirer of Mussolini, believer in the Divine Right of Kings and opponent of the 1944 Education Act. The winner will be announced in January. I can't wait.

— *Morning Star,* 26 May 2012

DREADFULLY OLD-FASHIONED: ON TRADITION AND COMMITMENT IN POLITICAL POETRY

For readers who are less familiar with your work, where would you position yourself politically and poetically?

I live in Middlesbrough, a large post-industrial town on the North-east coast, where for many years I taught in university adult-education. Since 1996, I have made a kind of living as a writer. I write metrically-exact, obsessively-rhyming, comic (I hope) verse in traditional English stanza-forms. I was a member of the British Communist Party until its demise in 1991.

In a sense, all my writing since then has been a kind of holding operation, holding the fort, trying to stop the sand blowing over the remains of the radical English poetic tradition until a younger generation can rediscover the necessity of democratic revolutionary change. So my political energies are now channelled almost entirely into cultural projects. These fall roughly into three categories.

First, the critical recovery of the British radical literary tradition, trying to keep books in print and writers in circulation. Second, community-based writing projects designed to hold open doors for other people to step through, so that they can access their experiences in their own words – working in prisons and schools, with recovering drug-addicts, children with behavourial difficulties, special needs etc. For many years I edited a weekly column of readers' poems in Middlesbrough's local paper, the *Evening Gazette*. In the 1990s I directed a community-writing festival on Teesside. Third, writing poetry.

You are a socially committed, politically active person. What made you take up poetry, of all things, to express your views – a form that many think will 'make nothing happen'? (Or putting the question differently: how and why did you begin? What was/is your driving motivation? What/who were/are your influences?)

I have been a member of CND for over thirty years, and was involved in the Yes campaign during the referendum for a Northern Assembly. But unfortunately, since the end of the CP

I have been politically isolated and woefully inactive. 'Politics' is once again the preserve of a tiny, wealthy elite; our only role is to legitimise their depradations by swelling the occasional crowd-scene for the evening news.

I still write a monthly poetry column for the *Morning Star* and I am still on the editorial board of *Socialist History*. But writing is a poor substitute for participating in civil society. Nevertheless, writing – especially writing poetry – allows me to say things that I cannot say in other ways. The other things I do – teaching, promoting and reviewing poetry, working in schools and prisons, running Smokestack, writing books for children – are simply ways of extending the conversation.

I grew up in a determinedly non-political, Methodist family. Although I left that world a very long time ago, my thinking is unavoidably shaped by that part of the Puritan moral vocabulary which requires us to bear witness, to testify on behalf of the speechless against the Pharisees, the powerful, the hypocrites and the liars. When I was a boy Christ's denunciation of the moneylenders in the temple never failed to excite me. The first poem I ever had published – at the age of eleven in the local newspaper – was a solemn little acrostic about the war in Biafra ('B for Biafra where there's bloodshed everywhere / I for the ignorance of people who don't care...'). My imagination is still patterned by the language of English Nonconformity – millenarian, Manichean and antinomian. The blurb on the back of *Nowhere Special* described it being located somewhere 'between pessimism of the intellect and the chiliasm of despair'. And of course all those years of standing in chapel and Sunday-school with a hymn book in my hand gave me an over-developed sense of rhythm, rhyme and stanza-form, of the power of metrical expectation and of a shared symbolic language.

At school we were expected to read some Betjeman and Hardy for O Level; although I am very fond of both poets now, they both left me completely cold then. At the same time, however, we were given some Catullus to translate as part of our Latin O Level. I had never read anything like it. After 'The Darkling Thrush' and 'Upper Lambourne' this was dynamite. Toxic stuff to give a sixteen year-old. It was a real revelation, and the point at which I think I knew I wanted to write poetry.

In your poetry, you cover vast political ground, from the politics of the private, the regional, the national to the global; from the political implications of digging up your patio to the lies of Bush and Blair. Are all of these levels inextricably intertwined or is there one, if you had to choose, at which you would expect political change to be most needed and poetry to be most effective?

I don't write about 'politics', certainly not about political parties, government legislation or parliamentary elections. But I am interested in the relationship between the powerful and the powerless, in the uses and abuses of power, and the ways in which the powerful maintain their positions and privileges. I do not think you have to be interested in politics to be repulsed by ludicrous and violent figures like Blair, Sarkozy, Bush, Brown, Berlusconi and Cameron. My definition of 'politics' in this sense would be something like St Paul's – 'For we do not wrestle only against flesh and blood, but against principalities, against powers, against the rulers of the darkness of this age, against spiritual hosts of wickedness in the heavenly places.'

In your poem 'There Was a Spirit in Europe', the speaker remarks 'The seeds of Change have shrunk to the belief / That nothing lasts and all things must decay.' This sounds rather bleak. How much despair can political poetry afford to voice before it defeats its own objective of striving for a better world?

It's a good question. But there is no point underestimating the serious of the situation. We still don't understand the extent to which progressive ideas and forces have been defeated, at least in Europe, in the last twenty years. The victory-march of the Right – economic libertarians, social authoritarians and violent imperialists – has been accompanied by the atrophying of the political process and the narrowing of democratic discourse. There is not much room for internationalism between the ugly nationalisms of the Far Right, the brutal supra-nationalism of the EU and the violent internationalism of globalisation. From the current European-wide assault on the social infrastructure to the air-strikes Libya, there is no alternative narrative to the triumphal history of the victors.

One of the attractive things about the British Communist Party was the sudden access of humility it enjoyed in its last years. While it was apparent to everyone that we no longer knew the answers, we were still interested in the questions. Anyone who thinks that a New Labour revival under Milliband is the answer, has forgotten what the question is.

'There was a Spirit in Europe' was written after a visit to a Partisan cemetery in Litakovo, Bulgaria. It was a wonderfully lonely and desolate place, prompting – as any cemetery can do – this kind of bleak contemplation. The poem is 'modelled' on Gray's 'Elegy Written in a Country Churchyard' ('The ploughman homeward plods his weary way,/ And leaves the world to darkness and to me'). The poem tries to tell the story of Frank Thompson, the British SOE officer and poet (and brother of Edward Thompson) executed with the Bulgarian partisans, whose fate may be said to illustrate, in miniature, the heroism, mendacity and tragedy of the Communist story.

We have to know the worst before we can imagine the best. And for anyone on the Left, especially the ex-Communist or post-Communist Left, we have to begin by acknowledging our contribution to the 'the worst'. Much of what you might consider my 'political' poetry is actually about the failure of utopianism. *Nowhere Special* was about the 'Fall' of 1990 (the title was partly a reference to Morris's *News from Nowhere*). *Three Men on the*

Metro (written with Bill Herbert and Paul Summers) explicitly addresses elements of Soviet history, its utopianism and its cynicism, its heroism and its crimes, its victories and its defeats. Although the British Communist Party was what its critics liked to call a Eurocommunist Party in its last decades, looking to Gramsci for inspiration rather than Lenin, this did not save us when the building collapsed in 1990. We were all implicated.

Does this mean that, in today's global political situation, it is easier to write political poems that are against things or that take stock of conditions than those in favour of, promoting, envisioning, alternative political models?

Yes. Poetry and politics are now expected to occupy separate, if not antagonistic worlds, like notions of the private and the public. Demotic language is now the poetry of advertising. Western societies are inoculated against the music of poetry just as much as they are against socialist or democratic ideas.

The great European communist poets of the twentieth-century – Ritsos, Aragon, Neruda, Hikmet, Vaptsarov, Alberti, Éluard, Hernandez, Vallejo, Brecht – lived in a period of rapid social and political change. They grew up in the newly-literate, urbanising societies of the early twentieth-century, characterised by new mass-media, mass politics and mass participation in civil society. Their writings were shaped first by their involvement in the early Modernist movements, and then by their rejection of Modernism, articulating more democratic ways of responding to the challenges of Modernity. Between them they lived through war, revolution, economic depression, Fascism, civil war, illegality, prison and exile. These were the circumstances out of which they created the most extraordinary body of work. While they may see unlikely ingredients in the creation of exceptional poetry, we can see now that it was these exceptional conditions that made them.

These poets made poetry out of politics and took politics into the worlds of poetry. They were able to write about the private and the public, the lyrical and the satirical, the utopian and the historical, combining documentary record, formal experimental and traditional forms. They were all (with the possible exception of Brecht) great love poets. They each celebrated the poetry of everyday life, of everyday objects – as Ritsos called it, 'the celestial side by side / with the everyday'. And they insisted on the poetry of ordinary language, demotic, colloquial speech. Above all, they found ways of synthesising the struggles for personal, political and national liberation as a single narrative – consider the poetry which Hikmet wrote in Istanbul and Bursa prisons, Brecht's 'Svendborg Poems', Neruda's *Canto General*, Aragon's *Le Crève-Coeur,* Vaptsarov's *Motor Songs,* or Ritsos's *Romiosini*. Of course the political circumstances today are wholly different. But the questions they tried to answer to still need asking again, in our own time, because we too need a new relationship between the intelligentsia and society, between writers and readers, between poetry and politics.

All great moments of popular resistance and struggle create their own poets. Poetry is uniquely placed to familiarise, popularise and mobilise ideas and feelings. It can combine memorable performance and quiet reflection, immediacy and enjoyment. And it can express a shared common-sense counter to the prevailing narratives of government and national media. There is a new spirit of resistance and rebellion abroad, a new generation mobilised by the anti-globalisation and anti-war movements. It is not yet Socialist, but it contains the potential for a revival of the Left, in spirit and in imagination. Poetry is still a way of saying things that cannot be said in other ways.

In how far has the field of political poetry in recent years already been touched by this new spirit? Has the scene become more vibrant and diverse or have there been sustained changes in the way certain issues are picked and treated by the poets? Almost all writers, it seemed, were and wrote against the war in Iraq – but this certainly does not mean that all of them were politically progressive.

The death of Adrian Mitchell has left the whole British poetry scene seriously weakened, including its critical, oppositional elements. Adrian was so well-loved, so popular (and such a great writer), he never had to whisper in order to be heard.

There was always a section of British intellectual opinion in thrall to Blair, just because he wasn't Thatcher or Major. But it is probably fair to say that there were no Blairite poets (even the then Poet Laureate, Andrew Motion, was eloquently critical of the illegal war in Iraq). The election of the Tories has simplified everybody's thinking. It is almost certainly true that there are no pro-Coalition poets presently writing poems in support of library closures, health service cuts, the continued occupation of Afghanistan or the current attack on Libya. The response to the recent Arts Council cuts has been led by the present poet laureate, Carol Ann Duffy.

Of course, this doesn't mean that everyone is writing about politics. It will take time for the attack on the infrastructure to knock down the high walls separating poetry and politics. But it will happen. Arts Council cuts to independent poetry presses like Arc, Enitharmon, Flambard and Salt, and to organisations like the Independent Publishers' Guild, the Poetry Trust, the Writers in Prison Network and the National Association of Writers in Education – while giving money to Faber and Faber – is going to seriously damage the already fragile economy of British poetry. What will happen to all those people with creative writing degrees? Finding a publisher is going to be harder than ever, never mind making a living from writing, Anger has to go somewhere.

Meanwhile there are plenty of British poets who (to quote from Smokestack's manifesto) are interested in the World as well as the Word, believe that poetry is a part of and not apart from society. For me, the most consistently rewarding poets writing at the moment are Ian McMillan, Ian Duhig, Paul Summers, Bill Herbert, Alistair Findlay, John Lucas, Peter Sansom, Katrina Porteous, George Szirtes, Tony Harrison, Linda France and John Hartley Williams. They are not in any sense a group, and they do not share an identifiable aesthetic, but each of these writers have found ways of what Brecht called 'singing about the dark times.' And I have recently learned a great deal from reading non-UK poets like Mahmoud Darwish, Francis Combes, Martin Espada, Salah Al Hamdani, Jim Scully, Fred Voss, Frank Reeve and Jacques Gaucheron.

You mentioned the Arts Council. In what ways do cultural institutions in your eyes inhibit political poetry in England?

British mainstream culture is very good at recognising what it already knows. But although it talks a lot about the 'new', the Next Big Thing usually turns out to be just like last year's dull model. I would say that most of the key institutions like the Poetry Society, the Poetry Book Society, the broadsheets, Front Row and the Forward Prize inhibit the writing of good poetry of any kind.

Just as the democratic process is increasingly blocked by political inertia, authoritarianism and deceit, the contemporary poetry scene chokes on self-promotion, literary celebrity and the travelling festival circus. And poets, readers and publishers are increasingly squeezed between Arts Council cuts, high-street monopolies, celebrity prizes, internet price-wars, Creative Writing battery-farms and book-signing festivals.

Hugo Williams, prize-winning poet and one of the judges for this year's Forward Prize, recently complained that there were too many entries this year. 'I think it's something to do with the democratisation of everything – that everyone's got a right to get a book out. I've got the feeling that sometimes it's more about desire than worth...' In a sense he was right. Poetry *is* about the 'democratisation of everything'. It's a way of extending the common ownership of experience, feeling and language. Poetry is a Republic, not a Meritocracy of the lucky, the talented or the privately-educated. It requires the proper humility necessary for any art. Maybe that's why it scares old Etonian cultural gate-keepers like Hugo Williams. And why contemporary British poetry is dying on its feet from boredom.

You suggest that poetry is a 'democratic act' and that it is the formal constraints, rules, and expectations of the genre that potentially sets off, rather than inhibits, the creativity of your students. Many would think, though, that it is the continued upholding and championing of certain of these and other cultural 'rules' that actually excludes and labels non-middle-class people as lacking in the first place. Just think of Anthony Easthope's verdict about the pentameter as 'a bourgeois national aspiration'. How do you deal with the ideological content with which some poetic forms have been invested in the course of history?

Language belongs to everyone. Writing – in the sense of the composition of memorable language to record events that need remembering – is historically a shared, collective, public activity. Poetry has only been written down in the last few hundred years. For most of human history it was mostly anonymous, passed on and learned and changed and passed on again. It is only in mass-literate societies that poetry becomes privatised, a personalised form of individual expression rather a means of public communication. Of course, mass-literacy does not mean equal access to literary or cultural power. The wooded slopes of Mount Parnassus are heavily protected by gamekeepers, armed with grammatical rules, unified spelling, critical standards, a canonical tradition and absurd arguments by people like Easthope (who never, as far as I know, wrote poetry).

When *Sticky* was published, the reviewer in *Tribune* dismissed the book's use of traditional forms as 'third rate Victorian verse. Unless you're writing for children or to be funny it does make the poetry look dreadfully old fashioned. Not many people, post Eliot, write like this any more...' There is a very interesting set of overlapping antagonisms here – writing for children, 'trying to be funny', and pre-Modern poetic forms (of course the reviewer made no mention of the book's arguments with New Labour).

For large parts of the twentieth-century – with important exceptions – rhyme was expelled from British poetry. On the whole, our best poets didn't use rhyme, or only used half-rhyme. Rhyme and metre were abandoned to popular song and advertising, and associated with amateur, uneducated and working-class poetry.

Where poets were once popularly understood to speak for and to the societies to which they belonged, the development of printing and publishing and the emergence of a reading-public has helped to elevate poets into a separate and professional caste. The Romantic idea of the rootless individual alienated from ordinary society (by education, sensibility and mobility) has become in our time the cult of the international poet as exile, crossing cultural, intellectual and linguistic borders. This cult reached its logical conclusion a few years ago with the Martian poets, who wrote about life on earth as if they really were aliens.

As a result, many people find contemporary poetry difficult. This is not usually the fault of the reader. It is partly an expression of the enduring elitism among British poets, for whom difficulty is an antidote to populism. It is partly a legacy of early twentieth-century Modernists like Eliot and Pound. In a complex and difficult world no-one wants to be accused of simplification. Moreover, poetry has to contend these days with other forms of expression, more clamorous and more powerful. The cult of 'difficulty' is one way in which poets feel they can be heard against the deafening white-noise of contemporary culture.

But poetry is essentially a means of communication, not a form of expression. Difficulty is only a virtue if the poem justifies the effort to understand it and you know that someone is listening. If poets think no-one is listening, they end up talking only to each other, or to themselves. And yet, stubbornly, subversively – wonderfully – the idea that poetry belongs to everyone who wants it still survives, for example in school playgrounds, working men's clubs, football grounds and prisons. Perhaps one of the reasons so many 'professional', prize-winning poets fear this other, older voice is that it is a reminder that the power of all art is still located in society, in the audience and not in the artist.

Much of the potential power of poetry still lies in its popular, traditional forms. The music of poetry can help to naturalise arguments which may seem outside the current narrow expectations of poetry. It can assert the longevity of these arguments, by placing them within older, popular literary traditions. Above all, this kind of writing can't easily be policed. It flies below the radar, a long way from the centres of cultural authority. The enemy can't follow. As a Venezuelan acquaintance once said to me, 'remember, every revolution is a poem, and every poem is a revolution...'

— from '"Dreadfully Old-Fashioned". On Tradition and Commitment in Political Poetry', in Uwe Klawitter and Claus-Ulrich Viol (eds) *Contemporary Political Poetry in Britain and Ireland* (Universitätsverlag Winter, 2013)

REVIEW OF KATRINA PORTEOUS, *TWO COUNTRIES*

Katrina Porteous is one of our best poets, and her big new book of poems *Two Countries* (Bloodaxe) is surely one of the most distinctive and important collections of 2015. It is certainly one of the most long-awaited. It almost twenty years since she published her last full-length collection, *The Lost Music,* about the decline of the fishing communities on the Northumbrian coast where she lives.

Two Countries brings together many of the poems she has written since then – commissions, community projects, collaborations with musicians and visual artists, variously published in magazines, newspapers, chapbooks, short-collections and anthologies.

It is worth buying this beautiful book for the texts of some of the extraordinary poems she has written for BBC Radio – notably 'This Far and No Further,' 'An Ill Wind', 'Borderers', 'Dunstanburgh', 'Durham Cathedral', 'Beach Ride,' 'When the Tide Comes' and 'The Refuge Box'.

Like the Radio Ballads of Charles Parker, AL Lloyd, Peggy Seeger and Ewan McColl, these long poems combine documentary footage, recorded speech, bird-song, folk-song, wind and weather, and a chorus of many layered voices. They draw on Border ballads, folklore, history, myth, geology, ornithology and memory, and employ a mixture of Standard English, Northumbrian dialect, Pitmatic and Border Scots.

Two Countries is a book about landscape and people 'and the conversation between them and their environment'. In many ways it is a book of elegies, solemn and fierce laments for the fishermen, hill farmers, lead-miners and boat-builders of Northumbria and Co Durham whose ways of living and working and speaking have been lost in our lifetimes:

> Once they capped the colliery shaft, it was goodbye
> ships and steel...
> Then the fishing fleet burned on the beach and it's

farewell all our boats:
And now it's the power to feed ourselves that's going
up in flames and smoke.

'Lost Names' is a simple litany of place-names, pits, jobs, birds and fishing cobles that have disappeared (Vane Tempest, redshank, hewer, oystercatcher, putter, The Lady Anne). As Porteous asks, 'Wha wad a thowt the world wad shrink sae quickly?'

The 'two countries' of the title are England and Scotland, both sides of Hadrian's Wall, both sides of the Tweed. But this is a book also about town and country, the traditional and the new, the pre-industrial and the post-industrial, about RP and Northern dialect, print and speech, class and alienation ('Aye hinny. It's a different country now').

On the one hand there is the daily struggle against the 'slant wind' and 'the sea's indifference'. On the other, there are the reivers – foot-and-mouth, deep-sea trawlers, Defra, the Common Agricultural and Fisheries policies and pit-closures:

The reivers have been and taken our sheep and cattle
And tied our hands,
And the brambles ravel like wires, and the fells
blacken
To No Man's Land.

Older than the reivers are the 'Romans':

The Romans came
Like a bunch of thieves,
Boned our land
Like a side of beef,
Built their camps
Where our steadings lay: /
It's the Romans get the plenty and the farmer pays...
Now regulations
Grow thick as weeds
And nobody asks us
And nobody agrees:
But when in Rome
It's the Roman way –
It's the Roman gets the plenty and the farmer pays.

If these poems are a record of change, they are also a hymn to what doesn't change – for example, the rooks in St Mary's churchyard in Seaham:

> Witnesses to Londonderry's riches,
> To the town's prosperity and the pitman's graft –
> Those dark tides of sons and fathers, leaving, returning
> From the pit shaft... they are onlookers
> To great catastrophes: wars, strikes; to private hearts
> Smashed like pebbles in the wreck of wave and water.

Above all, Porteous insists on the wisdom that survives 'From the slate to the keyboard':

> Not what we own
> But where we belong...
> Not what we buy
> But what we become
> Not what is consumed
> But what we keep building...
> Between the printed sand
> And the far horizon...
> Where we choose to sail
> Where we put out to sea.

— *Morning Star,* 29 November 2014

ANDY CROFT

THE PRIVATISATION OF POETRY

I am human, and nothing which is human can be alien to me.
— Terence

At the end of the fourth film in the 'Alien' franchise, *Alien Resurrection* (1997), the film's only two survivors are preparing to visit Earth. Although we have previously been told that it is a toxic 'shithole', one of them observes that from a distance the planet looks beautiful. 'I didn't expect it to be,' she says, 'what happens now?' The other gives a puzzled half-smile and shrugs, 'I don't know. I'm a stranger here myself.'

The 'stranger' is Ellen Ripley, who has been fighting the xenomorph aliens ever since Ridley Scott's original *Alien* (1979). Her bewildered description of herself as a 'stranger' is one of cinema's great understatements. For Ripley is a stranger, not only to a planet she has not seen for three hundred years, but also to herself. Ripley was killed at the end of the third film, and has been resurrected as a clone with part-alien DNA. She does not yet understand the extent of her humanity or know just how much of an alien she is.

All the human characters are dead at the end of *Alien Resurrection.* The film's only other survivor (played by Winona Ryder) is an android. Earlier in the film, when Ripley discovers that her companion is a robot, she observes, 'I should have known. No human being is that humane.' This is an idea that has been running through the series since *Aliens* (1986), when Ripley compares one of her companions to the aliens he is planning to sell to the Company's weapons division – 'I don't know which species is worse. You don't see them fucking each other over for a goddamn percentage...'

Alien Resurrection was a bleak *fin-de-siècle* farewell to a century of violence, avarice, fear and cruelty, and a grim welcome to a new millennium in which we are estranged from each other and from ourselves by exaggerated fears of differences. Ripley is a familiar figure in the twenty-first century – an alien, a homeless exile whose children are dead, a stranger in a strange land.

The phrase 'I'm a stranger here myself' is also a quotation from a song by Kurt Weill (another exile). Written with Ogden Nash for the 1943 Broadway hit *One Touch of Venus,* the song is a satirical comment on contemporary US life. In the musical, an ancient statue of the Greek goddess of sexual love (played by Mary Martin) comes alive in a New York museum. She is confused by the strangeness of the world in which she finds herself, especially by the apparent absence of love in the cold modern city:

> Tell me is love still a popular suggestion
> Or merely an obsolete art?
> Forgive me for asking, this simple question
> I'm unfamiliar with this part
> I am a stranger here myself.
>
> Please tell me, tell a stranger
> My curiosity goaded
> Is there really any danger
> That love is now out-moded?
>
> I'm interested especially
> In knowing why you waste it
> True romance is so freshly
> With what have you replaced it?

As a study in alienation, *One Touch of Venus* may not have been as hard-hitting as *The Threepenny Opera* or *Rise and Fall of the City of Mahagonny*, but it was nevertheless clearly shaped by Weill's experiences in Weimar Germany, where hysterical ideas about 'aliens' of course had catastrophic consequences. In the musical it is the non-human alien who understands more about human happiness than the human characters. It is not an exaggeration to say that Venus is both 'the heart of a heartless world', and an example of the commodification of desire in a society where 'all fixed, fast-frozen relations, with their train of ancient and venerable prejudices and opinions, are swept away... all that is solid melts into air, all that is holy is profaned.'

Which brings us to Marx's idea of *entfremdung*, the process by which, in class societies, we are alienated from Nature, from our work, from the products of our work, from each other and from ourselves. Each dramatic new stage of human social, economic and technological development has simultaneously pushed us farther apart from each other and from ourselves – property, slavery, money, territory, caste, class, religion, industrialisation, migration, urbanisation, mechanisation, militarisation, nationalism, empire, computerisation, globalisation...

Of course, we all experience this 'self-estrangement' differently. As Marx argued in *The Holy Family*, although 'the propertied class and the class of the proletariat present the same human self-estrangement,'

> the former class feels at ease and strengthened in
> this self-estrangement, it recognizes estrangement
> as its own power, and has in it the semblance of a
> human existence. The class of the proletariat feels
> annihilated, this means that they cease to exist in
> estrangement; it sees in it its own powerlessness and
> in the reality of an inhuman existence.

In a bewildering world where we feel ourselves to be strangers in our own lives, the false consolations of nostalgia, nationalism, chauvinism, religious fundamentalism and racism are tempting to many, especially to those with the least power. Each of these is an illusion 'which revolves around man as long as he does not revolve around himself' (during international football tournaments there is always a greater concentration of England flags in those parts of our cities with the smallest economic or political stake in British society). But fearing 'strangers' will not make the world less strange; attacking 'aliens' cannot mitigate our alienation from ourselves.

On the other hand, there are those forces that still pull us together – kinship, friendship, desire, solidarity, collectivity, utopianism, socialism. Despite all the commercial, cultural, social, economic and political pressures to emphasise our uniqueness and our separateness, the differences between us are not very great. We all share the same small planet, we breathe the same air and we share the same fate. And one of the ways in which we demonstrate and feel our common natures is through art. It is not just that creativity can raise individual 'self-esteem' or 'well-being'. All artistic creation, whether individual or collective, amateur or professional, private or public represents a kind of resistance to the complex, centrifugal forces that push us apart. Art is both a reminder of our co-operative origins and a promise of a collective future. Art can be many things – painting, dance, music, literature, sculpture, poetry – but it cannot be property. As soon as a work of art is owned by one individual it is not shared; if it is not shared, then it is not art.

Poetry in particular contains the potential to connect writers to readers, and readers to each other. It can help us feel a little more connected to each other than usual. When any poet stands up to read in public they have to address the readers outside the page, the listeners across the room and beyond. Poetry can remind us what is significant and help us to imagine what is important. It can help to naturalise ideas and arguments by placing them within popular literary traditions. Anticipation and memory implicate reader and listener in the making of a line or a phrase and therefore in the making of the argument. This establishes a potentially inclusive community of interest between the writer/speaker and the reader/ audience – through shared laughter, anger or understanding.

Writing – in the sense of the composition of memorable language to record events that need remembering – is essentially a shared, collective, public activity. Poetry is essentially a means of communication, not a form of self-expression. Difficulty is only a virtue if the poem justifies the effort to understand it. Why write at all, if no-one is listening? If they think no-one is listening, poets end up talking only to each other, or to themselves. As Adrian Mitchell once expressed it:

> In the days when everyone lived in tribes, poetry
> was always something which was sung and danced,
> sometimes by one person, sometimes by the whole
> tribe. Song always had a purpose – a courting song,
> a song to make the crops grow, a song top help or

instruct the hunter of seals, a song to thank the sun.
Later on, when poetry began to be printed, it took
on airs. When the universities started studying verse
instead of alchemy, poetry began to strut around like
a duchess full of snuff. By the middle of the twentieth
century very few British poets would dare to sing.

It seems to me that this is still understood at a subterranean level within British society, a long way from the centres of cultural authority and the cult of the 'new'. Poets like Linton Kwesi Johnson, Kokumo, Moqapi Selassie, Benjamain Zephaniah and Jean Binta Breeze do not read their poems in public – they *sing* them. The most distinctive feature of an Urdu-Punjabi *musha'ara* (a marathon poetry-reading) is the level of audience participation. Poets do not always read their 'own' work. They often sing. They are frequently interrupted by applause, by requests for a line to be read again, by the audience joining in the reading of well-known poems. And *musha'ara* attract hundreds of people of all ages.

There is something comparable about the role of poetry inside prison. Men who would not often go near a library in their ordinary lives, in prison can find solace and encouragement in reading and writing poetry. Prison magazines always carry pages of poetry. The Koestler Awards are an important part of the prison calendar. No-one is embarrassed to say that they like poetry in prison. There are certain poems – usually about love, heroin and regret – that prisoners take with them from one prison to another, copying them out and learning them by heart until the poems 'belong' to them.

In other words, the idea that language – and therefore poetry – belongs to everyone, is still felt most vividly among those who have been historically excluded from education and literacy by the forces of caste and class, empire and slavery.

The French Marxist philosopher Alain Badiou has argued that it is not a coincidence that most of the great poets of the twentieth-century were communists (Hikmet, Brecht, Neruda, Eluard, Ritsos, Vallejo, Faiz, MacDiarmid, Aragon, Mayakovsky, Alberti, Darwish, Sanguineti, etc). For Badiou, there exists 'an essential link between poetry and communism, if we understand "communism" closely in its primary sense':

> the concern for what is common to all. A tense, paradoxical, violent love of life in common; the desire that what ought to be common and accessible to all should not be appropriated by the servants of Capital. The poetic desire that the things of life would be like the sky and the earth, like the water of the oceans and the brush fires on a summer night – that is to say, would belong by right to the whole world... it is first and foremost to those who have nothing that everything must be given. It is to the mute, to the stutterer, to the stranger, that the poem must be offered, and not to the chatterbox, to the grammarian, or to the nationalist. It is to the proletarians – whom Marx defined as those who have nothing except their own body capable of work – that we must give the entire earth, as well as all the books, and all the music, and all the paintings, and all the sciences. What is more, it is to them, to the proletarians in all their forms, that the poem of communism must be offered.

Of course, there are always forces pulling poets in the other direction. Like everything else, poetry is a contested space. The broadsheets, the BBC and most literary festivals are dominated by corporate publishers and a celebrity star-system. The whole apparatus of arts-coverage by press-release, celebrity book-festivals, short-lists, awards and prize-giving ceremonies seems almost designed to alienate as many people as possible from poetry – except as consumers. The result is the victory march of Dullness, characterised by humourlessness, political indifference, a disregard for tradition, a serious underestimation of poetry's music and a snobbish hostility to amateurs. And all decorated in the usual language of PR disguised as literary criticism ('sexy', 'dark', 'sassy', 'edgy', 'bold', 'daring' etc).

Last year I published, at Smokestack Books, a collection of poems by the Newcastle writer Sheree Mack. Sheree's mother is of Ghanaian and Bajan ancestry; her father is from Trinidad. *Laventille* told the story of the 1970 Black Power Revolution in

Trinidad and Tobago, when for forty-five days an uprising of students, trade unions and the disaffected poor threatened to overthrow the government. It was a courageous and beautiful book, an original attempt to combine history and poetry as a 'shrine of remembrances' for the ordinary people behind the headlines.

A few weeks after the book was published Sheree found herself accused of borrowing phrases without attribution from other poets. Most were happy to see elements of their work resurrected and re-made like this, but a few were not. Although I variously offered to insert erratum slips in the book, to reprint the book with the necessary acknowledgements, and to print a new version of the book without the poems in question, Sheree's accusers seemed more interested in mobilising a howling mob on social-media, armed with the usual pitchforks and burning torches. There followed several weeks of extraordinary personal abuse directed at author and publisher, a feature on *Channel 4 News*, demands that Sheree should be stripped of her qualifications and sacked from her teaching job, an editorial in *Poetry News,* and threats of legal action from two corporate publishers. Several festivals withdrew invitations for Sheree to read from the book. Eventually the book was withdrawn from sale and pulped.

I do not believe for a minute that Sheree intended to 'steal' anyone else's work. Some of her borrowings were so obvious that they did not need acknowledging (any more than her poem called 'What's Going On?' did not need to spell out its debt to Marvin Gaye). 'Laventille Love Song' for example, did not attempt to disguise its debt to Langston Hughes' 'Juke Box Love Song'. The point of the poem was to throw together two different moments in Black history, dialectically linked by the deliberate echoes of one poem in the other.

Sheree's fault was one of omission and carelessness; the reaction of her accusers was deliberate, hysterical and disproportionate. Sheree made no attempt to conceal her borrowings, she did not profit from them, she has apologised for them repeatedly and she has been excessively punished. No-one has lost anything – except a sense of proportion and decency. Sheree's faults may be forgiven; the venom of her pursuers is unforgiveable. And a beautiful, revolutionary book has been lost.

I am not interested in calculating how many words a poet may borrow from another writer without being accused of 'theft', or swapping examples of successful plagiarists – most notably, of course, Shakespeare, Stendhal and Brecht. (For the record, my last three books were comic verse-novels based on *Hamlet, Nineteen Eighty-four* and *Don Juan.*) But I am fascinated by the moral panic around 'intellectual property' in the contemporary poetry world, in the way that notions of private property have entered the world of poetry.

Property is a very recent (and contested) innovation in human history, usually used to determine access to scarce or limited resources such as land, buildings, the means of production, manufactured goods and money. It is a shifting concept; not so long ago, women, children and slaves were subject to property law; today we have 'copyright', 'intellectual property', 'identity theft' and 'image rights'.

There are three kinds of property – common property (where resources are governed by rules which make them available for use by all or any members of the society), collective property (where the community as a whole determines how important resources are to be used), and private property (where contested resources are assigned to particular individuals).

It is difficult to see how the many various elements of any poem – words, phrases, grammatical structures, rhyme and metre, emotional syntax, allusions, echoes, patterns, imagery and metaphor etc – can be described as 'property' in any of the above senses (except perhaps 'common property'). None of these elements are scarce or finite; their use by one person does not preclude their use by any number of others. In an age of mechanical reproduction, it is not possible to 'steal' a poem or part of a poem, only to copy it.

All poetry inhabits the common language of everyday living. A poem can be unique without being original; it can be 'new' at the same time that it is already known. Most important human activities are not subject to ideas of ownership. Talking, walking, whistling, running, making love, speaking a foreign language, cooking, playing football, baking bread, dancing, conversation, knitting, drawing – these are all acquired skills which we learn by imitating others, but they are not subject to ideas of ownership.

Historically, poetry was always understood to be much closer to these than to those things that the law regards as 'property' (land, money etc). No-one in, say fourteenth-century Italy would have understood the idea of 'stealing' a poem. Most cultures, even today, regard poetry as 'common property'. You don't hear many 'original' poems at an Urdu-Punjabi *musha'ara*. Everyone borrows/steals/copies/appropriates poetry in prison. Which is another way of saying that everyone owns it. And if everyone owns it, there is nothing to steal.

Until very recently in human history, poets were popularly understood to speak for and to the societies to which they belonged. The development of printing and publishing and the emergence of a reading-public have helped to elevate poets into a separate and professional caste. The Romantic idea of the sensitive individual alienated from ordinary society (by education, sensibility and mobility) has become in our time the cult of the international poet as exile, crossing cultural, intellectual and linguistic borders. This cult reached its logical conclusion a few years ago with the Martian poets, who wrote about life on earth as if they really were aliens.

The current moral panic over 'plagiarism in poetry' seems to derive from several overlapping elements – the post-Romantic privatisation of feeling and language, the fetishisation of 'novelty' in contemporary culture, half-hearted notions of intellectual property, the long-term consequences of Creative Writing moving from university adult education onto campus as an academic subject, the creation of a large pool of Creative Writing graduates competing for publication, jobs and prizes and the decline in the number of poetry publishers. If poetry is privatised, a personalised form of individual expression rather a means of public communication, then it needs to be policed by ideas of copyright, grammatical rules, unified spelling, critical standards and a canonical tradition.

The witch-hunting of Sheree Mack was an instructive episode in the internal workings of intellectual hegemony. The corporate lawyers and national media only joined the chase after a handful of poets (most of whom had not read *Laventille*) had already attacked one of their own, in the name of economic forces which are inimical to poetry.

Poetry arises out of the contradictions and consolations of a whole life and a whole society. It requires the proper humility necessary for any art. Poetry is not a Meritocracy of the educated, the privileged or the lucky. It is a Republic. Poetry is indivisible. If it doesn't belong to everybody, it is something else – show business, big business, self-promotion, attention-seeking, *property*. As Alain Badiou argues:

> Poets are communist for a primary reason, which is absolutely essential: their domain is language, most often their native tongue. Now language is what is given to all from birth as an absolutely common good. Poets are those who try to make a language say what it seems incapable of saying. Poets are those who seem to create in language new names to name that which, before the poem, has no name. And it is essential for poetry that these inventions, these creations, which are internal to language, have the same destiny as the mother tongue itself: for them to be given to all without exception. The poem is a gift of the poet to language. But this gift, like language itself, is destined to the common – that is, to this anonymous point where what matters is not one person in particular, but all, in the singular. Thus, the great poets of the twentieth century recognized the grandiose revolutionary project of communism something that was familiar to them – namely that, as the poem gives its inventions to language and as language is given to all, the material world and the

world of thought must be given integrally to all, becoming no longer the property of a few but the common good of humanity as a whole.

— *Culture Matters,* 2015

PLAGIARISM IN POETRY: INTERVIEW WITH ROBERT FARRELL

Is there a difference between allusion and plagiarism?

The difference seems to be measured simply by the varying noise levels of approval or outrage. If readers and reviewers think that they recognise most of the sources that inform the work of a well-known writer, then they are applauded as 'allusive', 'inter-textual' and 'ludic'. Anything else is 'plagiarism'.

I have never been remotely interested in 'plagiarism' scandals, which always seem to me to demean everyone involved, like excitable children accusing each other of copying. All poets writing in English use the same language, the same alphabet and the same grammatical structure. We are all inheritors of the same literary traditions. We all drink from the same well. No poet should be so lacking in humility as to think that they can ever write anything that is 'original'. All any of us can ever hope to do is to restate in a contemporary idiom what has already been said, probably by much better poets than we can ever be. An original poem is as impossible as an original colour. Which is perhaps why, for all the current emphasis on poets finding their 'voice', so many contemporary poets sound the same...

The intellectual content of a poem may be a slightly different issue. But how many poets can you think of whose work is intellectually 'original'? And how many original ideas do any of us ever have? Unless you are Galileo, Newton, Darwin, Marx or Einstein, I think it is probably wise not to demand that other people should be original in their thinking. Anyway, the achievement of even these men would have been impossible without the work of their predecessors; as Newton put it, 'if I have seen further, it is by standing on the shoulders of giants.' In the circumstances, it seems to me that those poets who gaily accuse others of lacking 'originality' should look again at their own work with a bit more humility.

Perhaps we can return to the question of originality later. But let's grant for the moment that originality in any form isn't possible and agree that all we can do is restate what has already been said. Doesn't the hope to which you point – to 'restate' existing ideas in new language, to see further than our predecessors – imply that a poet can fail to restate what's already been said and simply repeat it? That he or she can fail to 'see further' and rather see the same thing as another poet and call it new? Milton in his Eikonclastes wrote, 'For such kind of borrowing as this, if it be not better'd by the borrower, among good Authors is accounted Plagiarie.' If you don't want to call inept or inartistic borrowing 'plagiarism,' I can accept that. Perhaps we could agree to call it a bad poem or say it's not poem at all or that it (or the best part of it) is someone else's poem. In any case, don't poets (or 'poets') who liberally borrow from other poets and fail to improve on the original fail at the thing you seem to think a poem at the very least should do?

Yes, of course. The fear of repeating oneself, never mind other people, must be a constant for all writers. But notions of 'originality' are relative. I have spent too many years working in primary schools and in prisons not to know that what may seem derivative, clichéd, tired or borrowed to some readers, can feel like an exciting and original achievement to others. The ability to 'see further than our predecessors' is largely dependent on education and cultural access. A cliché is only a cliché if you have read it before. In one sense, the making of any poem, no matter how clumsy or derivative, is to be celebrated. As the Chilean poet Nicanor Parra put it, 'In poetry everything is permitted. // With only this condition of course, / You have to improve the blank page.' How many of us can confidently say to ourselves that we always do that?

Are there different kinds of plagiarism? If so, are some forms of plagiarism better, more creative, or more interesting than others? Are there forms that are less creative or interesting in your view?

The work that goes into writing any poem is impossible to quantify. First, there is a life-time of reading, thinking, listening, talking and understanding; second, the conscious effort to concentrate an idea, fix a memory or crystallise a feeling in words; third, the patient struggle with the organisation, shape and form of the words on the page and the sound of their music in your head; fourth, a series of critical judgements as to when the work is finished; fifth, an evaluation of the poem's likely relationship with other readers. Buried somewhere inside all this are the various stages at which the poet consciously and unconsciously uses their various source materials, internal and external. Who can judge which part of the process, or which versions, are more 'creative' than others? Who cares? The only question that should concern us, is whether a poem is as good as it can be, given the circumstances of the writer, the writing and its reception.

So are you saying that readers of poetry can't draw from established critical standards (of whatever sort) or form new standards in order to evaluate the quality of poetry? It seems disingenuous to imply that every poem is as good as every other poem as long as it's 'as good as it can be.' A good limerick is a good limerick, but I don't think many people would agree that a good limerick, however good, is as good as a good sestina. Analogously, there are better and worse examples of poetic borrowing and more skilful – more artful – ways of drawing on our shared poetic past or from contemporary works. Many poets who borrow lines, ideas, or images and wish to do so skilfully include notes in their books that indicate their sources, especially if those sources are less well known. Does a poet have the obligation to 'cite' her sources in some way if she is borrowing material? Is there a certain amount of material or threshold that warrants acknowledgement, particularly if the source is contemporary?

There are so many obstacles between any poem and any reader; signposts on the page like title, epigraph, acknowledgement, glossary etc can only help. Unless of course, they are too obvious, distracting or cumbersome. I am not interested in calculating how many words a poet may borrow from another writer without being accused of 'theft', or swapping examples of successful plagiarists – most notably, of course, Shakespeare, Stendhal and Brecht. And just for the record, my last three books were comic verse-novels based on *Hamlet, Nineteen Eighty-four* and *Don Juan.*

Clearly in the present climate everyone has to be careful to cover their backs to avoid being dragged into the next public row with the self-appointed commissars now sniffing around the poetry world for unattributed borrowings. A few months ago, at a book-launch in Nottingham, I read a new poem of mine called 'The Sailors of Ulm'. Before doing so I explained that the poem is supposed to 'echo' Louis MacNeice's 'Thalassa', and that the title refers to Lucio Magri's history of the PCI, *Il Sarto di Ulm,* which itself was a reference to Brecht's poem 'The Tailor of Ulm'. By way of apology for such a laboured introduction, I joked that I was covering myself in case there was anyone in the audience from the poetry-police. The following day one of the principal witch-hunters in the *Laventille* affair (who was not there) e-mailed the organisers of the reading to ask if he could confirm that I had insulted the poetry police.

But how do you argue that a good sestina is 'better' than a limerick? The world is full of entertaining limericks and dull, clanking sestinas. I can think of many occasions when I would rather read a good limerick than a sestina. And if anyone doubts the value of a good limerick, I can do no better than recommend *The Limerickiad*, Smokestack Books' three volume (soon to be four) raucous, clever history of Eng Lit in limericks by Martin Rowson.

Anyway, who is comparing? What is the point of the comparison? In what way is a sestina 'better' than a limerick? What is the measure? The amount of time needed to read them? The amount of ink required to write them? If a sestina is 'better' than a limerick, how does it compare to a villanelle? I have always found terza rima difficult to write, but ottava rima enjoyable to read; so how can I say which form is 'better'? Is anyone prepared to argue that the iambic foot used in most sestinas is superior to the amphibrach of the limerick? Or are we making a judgement about the relative seriousness of the subject-matter usually carried by the two forms? But who says that light-verse is inferior to 'heavy' verse? This sounds like the old university senior common-room game of Golden Poets and Silver Poets, Major and Minor, Gentlemen and Players. The pressure to evaluate and grade poems and poets seems to me to be both unattractive and pointless. What is 'better', a motorbike or a banana? It depends if you are in a hurry or if you are hungry.

I think the Milton quote referred to earlier might clear Shakespeare, Stendahl, and Brecht from the label of plagiarist and I'm assuming whatever source materials you drew from for your verse novel, 1948, were in some way skilfully acknowledged. But to return to your answer to the previous question, there seem to be many people who care whether large or small portions of other peoples' poems end up in another poet's work, namely poets who find their work published under another person's name. Let's pose a hypothetical situation and consider 1948. I notice that both you and the illustrator of the book retained your copyright. Would you be comfortable with someone reprinting unattributed portions of the book under their name or repurposing the images in an uncreative context (i.e. not as part of a new work of art that transforms the source material but 'as is' or with slight modification) without attribution?

The copyright statement inside *1948* was put in by the publisher. If somebody seriously wanted to copy some or all of the 150 *onyeginskaya* sonnets in *1948* I would be flattered. First of all it would mean that someone had read the damn thing! Secondly it would presumably mean that they had enjoyed the book enough to want to do this. And if they were able to 'improve' on the original then good luck to them. It certainly won't earn them any money!

My impression is that those who are most outraged by revelations or accusations of plagiarism in the poetry world are not usually the 'victims', but other would-be writers who feel that their own route to literary success is suddenly compromised. What is the point of spending all those years on Creative Writing programmes developing their unique 'individual' voice if it turns out that it is not to so exclusively theirs after all?

A follow up to the previous question: How do you handle copyright at your own press? Most Creative Commons licenses require at the minimum attribution credit for material designated for reuse or repurposing. But they do have a 'No Rights Reserved' option (CC0). Would you consider publishing your work or the work of your authors under a 'No Rights Reserved' Creative Commons license? Would your authors be comfortable with seeing their poems published in a journal under another poet's name?

I don't know – I'm not a lawyer! I have run Smokestack Books for twelve years single-handedly and unpaid. In this time I have published 110 titles and sold almost 30k books. I do not have the time, the energy, or the interest to pursue this kind of stuff about copyright. All Smokestack titles carry the usual statement about the author retaining copyright to their work. As far as I am concerned it is a formality. If I am approached by an editor who wants to include a poem by a Smokestack author in an anthology I pass this request to the poet.

Let's shift topics for a minute. To what degree does the economic structure of the 'poetry business' – a structure which may lead a poet to feel pressured to produce a certain amount or certain kind of work in order to secure grants or academic employment -- contribute to what your average person might call poetic plagiarism (an instance in which a poet takes another poet's work and with little or no modification and claims authorship)?

The narrow economics of the contemporary poetry scene in the UK undoubtedly encourages the idea of poetry as property. This seems to me to be a wholly pernicious idea, inimical to genuine creativity. It derives in part from the way that the broadsheets, the BBC, the corporate festivals and the prize-giving circus create and maintain a hierarchy of poets (and a hierarchical idea of poetry) based on the lists of corporate publishers. It is also a result of the way that so many poets much further down the food chain these days make a poor living as part-time Creative Writing teachers in universities.

It is worth remembering that Creative Writing in the UK emerged as an academic subject a long time before universities realised that they could make money out of it. When I worked for Leeds University in the early 1980s, I was told that I couldn't teach Creative Writing because it was not a 'proper academic subject'. Eventually I was permitted to teach it, but only as part of a special programme of free courses designed for unemployed people in Middlesbrough (a long way from the university). Of course, Leeds University, like all UK universities, now runs undergraduate and post-graduate degree programmes in Creative Writing. But I don't imagine that many unemployed people can afford them.

The origins of Creative Writing in the UK lie a long way from Higher Education – in Adult Education, Women's Education, community arts and organisations like the Federation of Worker Writers and Community Publishers. The sudden and distorting presence of the universities in the poetry economy has brought with it the imported ideas of intellectual property, critical hierarchies, career-structures as well as the instincts of corporate lawyers.

If poetry is a commodity, it needs to be policed (grammatical rules, unified spelling, critical standards, canonical tradition etc). And before it can be sold, it has to be owned (copyright and intellectual property etc). There is a direct connection, I think, between the commodification of poetry and the privatisation of poetry as a personalised form of individual expression rather a means of public communication.

Hold on now! Poets have proclaimed their originality and criticized others for taking credit for their or other poets' work (in whole or in part) since antiquity. But, again, let's stay with the current topic and restate this last question. Does the poet who chooses to be a part of the of the contemporary 'poetry business,' a business which is predicated on the traffic of poems that contain 'the original 'voice' of the poet,' as you put it, or of the deliberate (and acknowledged) subversion of such 'voice' poems, have the obligation to make clear what it is that they are purveying within that marketplace?

No. Poetry is not a marketplace and a poem is not a commodity to be bought and sold. In the UK a chain of opticians is currently claiming legal ownership over the word 'Should've', while a Danish brewery apparently owns the copyright to the word 'probably'. This is ludicrous. Poets should have nothing to do with this kind of thinking.

Historically, poetry was always understood to be much closer to these than to those things that the law regards as 'property' (land, money etc). No one in, say, fourteenth-century Italy would have understood the idea of 'stealing' a poem. Most cultures, even today, regard poetry as 'common property'. Which is another way of saying that everyone owns it. And if everyone owns it, there is nothing to steal.

Poets in fourteenth century Italy would definitely have understood the idea of stealing a poem, although what they thought was important was the formal structure of the canzone. 'Theirs was a literature that strove for originality of form almost above all else,' Chambers notes in his Introduction to Old Provencal. As an example of this concern, he quotes elsewhere in his book the 12th century troubadour Peire d'Alvernhe's line, 'never was a song good or of any value which resembled the songs of another.'

But I think that it would be rather difficult to write a history of, say, Blues or Folk Music in these terms. And there are many poetic traditions – Urdu for example – which rely very heavily on shared phrases and commonly used figures of speech.

Anyone who enjoys generic fiction will tell you that part of the pleasure of this kind of reading is the recognition of its familiar patterns. Not many readers of westerns or hospital romances, for example, will thank an author for radically disrupting their expectations of the form.

One of the reasons I write almost entirely in traditional stanzas – metrically precise, rhymingly obsessive, formal straight-jackets – is the creation of a shared, anticipated music with the listener. It is like joining a traditional dance with complicated steps that everyone knows. This only works if each new song in some way 'resembles' the songs of others.

But I'm glad you brought up this period of literary history because I think it prompts a really interesting question about the complicated relationship throughout history between authorship and originality and ownership and 'the marketplace,' however we define that. We find these complications in Greece in Pindar's work and at Rome in Martial's (who first brought the notion of 'plagiary' – kidnapping – into a literary context). We find it the Renaissance when the word 'plagiary' first enters English. And of course we find it today.

Whether we want to call it originality or not, authorship and being recognized as the author of a work seems to be central to poets' self-understanding to this day, even among the Communist poets you refer to in your essay and among those who largely agree with your points about language and poetry. A case in point might be the American novelist Jonathan Lethem, who was interviewed after the publication of his excellent essay, 'The Ecstasy of Influence,' which makes many of the same points you've made about language, the commons, and the impossibility of writing anything fully original. In an interview following it (forgive the long quote), he clarified his views on originality, saying, 'I think originality is a word of praise for things that have been expressed in a marvelous way and that make points of origin for any particular element beside the point.

When you read Saul Bellow or listen to Bob Dylan sing, you can have someone point to various cribbings and it won't matter, because something has been arrived at which subsumes and incorporates and transcends these matters. In that way, sourcing and originality are two sides of the same coin, they're a nested partnership.' He goes on to expand on what he means by 'originality' by relating it to the notion of 'surprise': 'You want to feel surprised. If my description proposes some sort of dutiful, grinding, crossword puzzle work – 'let me take some Raymond Chandler here and graft it to some Philip K. Dick over here' – that's horrendous. You, the author, want to experience something that feels surprising and uncanny and native. You want to take all your sourcing and turn it into an experience that – for you first and foremost, and then of course for the reader – feels strong or urgent in a way that mimics some kind of natural, automatic process.'

All of this leads me to a two-part question. First, as opposed to what we might call a 'strong' notion of originality, one that sees authors as capable of coming up with wholly original thoughts and expressions over which they can claim total ownership, Lethem seems to be putting forward what we might call a 'weak' notion of originality, one that emphasizes the author's ability to surprise herself and us regardless of source material. I'm interested in what you might think of Lethem's take on the word 'originality,' which in spirit seems to be not that far from Milton.

Second, from the perspective of Lethem's 'weak' notion of originality, it seems like you're conflating 'strong' notions of 'originality' and 'ownership' – possessiveness over property rights – with 'authorship' and 'originality' in the weaker sense – surprisingly marvelous writing and the pride that comes with such accomplishment. You criticize those who decry plagiarism as defenders of private property because you believe that a poem is not a commodity that can be bought or sold and that it's on these strong grounds that they base their objections. But is it fair to say that it's on those grounds that most people find the plagiarist pathetic? Mightn't the objectors to plagiarism/inept borrowing/bad poems (however we want to describe unsurprising writing) be objecting to the plagiarist's false (and rather sad) claims of authorship and his implicit denial of others' surprising achievements (however modest) rather than any violation of notions of ownership?

I like the concept of 'surprising' writing, although it has to be said British literary culture seems interested only in 'unsurprising' writing at the moment. I don't know Jonathan Lethem's work, or this essay, but it sounds like a very useful account of my sense of the way I write. During the two days we have been conducting this conversation by e-mail, I have also been writing an obituary, proof-reading a children's novel, copy-editing an anthology of poetry and trying to finish a poem about the refugee crisis in Europe. I have also written about sixty e-mails and half a dozen letters. But I don't think that it is true to say that I have been exercising a 'weak' originality for most of the time and saving my 'strong' originality only for the poem (especially as it borrows, self-consciously, some phrases from Byron's *Childe Harold*). Or does such deliberate – and irreverent – borrowing represent a kind of 'strong' originality in itself? Which kind of 'originality' are you and I using in this conversation?

And why should the poetry world suddenly be the focus of these questions about *ownership*. Why now? Why poetry? Why not the worlds of, say, ventriloquism, athletics, topiary or pottery? Who benefits from the importation of this legal vocabulary into poetry? If there were any money involved it would be tragic. But considering the tiny amounts of money that anyone ever earns from poetry in the UK, there is something grimly comical about poets accusing each other of stealing something which belongs to everyone.

— *The Argotist Online,* 2016

STRIPPED NAKED BY THE FLAMES

I have never seen so many people at a poetry festival, so many television cameras – or so many Kalashnikovs. Two years ago I was in the southern Iraqi city of Basra with my friends the poets Amarjit Chandan and Abdulkareem Kasid. We were guests of the Iraqi Writers Union for the thirteenth annual Al-Marbed international poetry festival.

Dedicated to the late Iraqi poet and communist Mehdi Mohammad Ali, the festival attracted almost a hundred poets, amateurs and professionals, from Morocco, Tunisia, Egypt, Bahrain, Yemen, Iran, Kuwait, Sudan, Iraq, Assyria, Lebanon, Syria and the Iraqi diaspora scattered across the world.

During a week of readings and debates, poetry and music, we visited the birthplace of Basra's most famous poet Badr Shakir al-sayyab, as well as the Basra international football stadium. There was a showing of the film *Samt al-Rai/The Silence of the Shepherd* introduced by its director Raad Mushatat. One of the festival readings took place on the Shat al-Arab waterway, on board a river-boat built for Saddam Hussein.

But the festival was taking place in a deadly context. Iraqi forces were still fighting Daesh/ISIS in the north. The billboards by the side of the roads advertised, not consumer-goods, but the faces of young men from Basra who had died fighting Daesh. Each night we were woken by the sound of gunfire marking the repatriation of local boys killed fighting in Mosul.

With a heavily armed security presence at all the readings, it was hardly surprising that the festival was a serious-minded affair. Most of the poets recited long poems, often from memory and usually about the suffering and grief of the Iraqi people. One man read a poem about the death of his son, killed fighting in Fallujah. Another compared Iraqi children to a forest of young trees cut down before they are full grown. One poet observed that every Iraqi child has an older brother called Death. Another described the poor of the world as the fuel that keeps the endless fires of war burning. There was a long poem about a local teacher who was badly injured by a Daesh car-bomb; although she managed to crawl out of the car, she realised that her clothes were on fire and that her modesty before God was threatened, so she climbed back into the burning car to die.

In the circumstances, the banner in the Basra International Hotel declaring that 'Poetry is the Present and Future of Basra' was a defiant assertion of the enduring importance of poetry in Iraqi society, its relationship to shared ideas of nation, faith, language and history. Arabic poetry has a 'yearning' music, descending cadences and distinct metrical patterns, each intended for a different emotional delivery, and designed to invite audience participation. At some of the evening readings there were over a thousand people, men and women, young and old, frequently interrupting the poets with shouts and gestures of appreciation and applause. A six year-old boy recited, entirely from memory, a ten minute-long poem comparing Iraq to a grieving woman.

The idea of a publicly-owned, serious and shared poetic tradition clearly persists across all classes in Arab culture. Television shows like *Million's Poet* and *Prince of Poets* regularly attract millions of viewers. Writers like Mahmoud Darwish, Adonis, Badr Shakir al-Sayyab and Ahmed Shawki are known and their poetry enjoyed by audiences a long way beyond the world of literature, and beyond the limits of literacy.

According to ALESCO (the Arab League Educational, Scientific and Cultural Organisation), 27% of people in the Arab world cannot read or write. Six million Iraqis – 20% of the population – are illiterate. But poetry is older than literacy; its historical role is to say in memorable ways those things which society needs to hear and to remember. It is only in mass-literate societies that poetry becomes diminished in importance and seriousness.

In the UK – the world's first mass-literate society – writing has long been professionalised. The result is the commodification of poetry, the privatisation of feeling and the high educational entry-requirements of our cultural institutions. Large parts of the contemporary British poetry 'industry' are embarrassingly trivial and self-important, characterised by snobbery, narcissism, humourlessness and political indifference.

Despite the ritual assertions of poetry's popularity – 'Brits have rekindled their love of verse,' 'the Cinderella of literary forms is back,' 'Poetry sales soar as political millennials search for clarity,' 'A new generation of female writers has attracted millions of online followers and an increasingly diverse audience,' 'With soaring sales and a younger, broader audience, poetry is on a high,' etc – sales of poetry books last year represented less than 0.7% of all book sales in the UK.

Every January the broadsheets announce the best books that are going to be published in the coming twelve months. Of course, no-one has read all these books, since most of them have not yet been published (several do not even have titles). Nor, it is fair to assume, has anyone read all the tens of thousands of unpublished books that are *not* on these lists. The *Guardian*'s 'Best Books of 2017' included only eight poetry books – all but two of which were from Faber's catalogue. The paper's 'literary calendar' for 2018 managed to include just seven books of poetry (out of a recommended list of 92 titles); this year the *Guardian* could only find nine poetry books worth including on their list of the 152 books 'you'll be reading this year'.

But the gate-keeping institutions intent on discovering the next poetry revival seem to be rather less interested in poetry than they are in poets. The most notable aspect of the row following Rebecca Watts' review of Hollie McNish's *Plum* in these pages is that both the *Guardian* and Radio Four saw it as a *news story about poets* rather than an arts-story about poetry and literary criticism ('Poetry world split over polemic').

While corporate publishers compete to establish a hierarchy of poets based on their own lists, angry mobs squabble on social-media over the ownership of poetry. The result is a kind of privatisation-grab and a closing down of debate and enquiry.

This has been exacerbated by the recent and somewhat unlikely involvement of Higher Education institutions (during one of the recent plagiarism rows a friend told me that was forbidden from expressing an opinion on any of the issues involved, by the legal department of the university where he teaches).

National Poetry Day is less a celebration of poetry than of the PR machinery of corporate publishers. As Michael Schmidt has argued, 'poetry prizes are now the vehicle of literary reception. Control the prizes and you control the culture of reception'. The apparatus of celebrity book-festivals, 'controversial' short-lists and prize-giving ceremonies is designed to guarantee access to the financial rewards of poetry (commissions, contracts, festivals, university teaching posts, more prizes, etc).

The news drama around these prizes usually follows the same creaking narrative of major names, newcomers, bookies' favourites, outsiders and dark-horses. This has recently been enlivened by rows about identity ('TS Eliot prize row: is winner too young, beautiful – and Chinese?', 'Ode to whiteness: British poetry scene fails diversity test', 'Forward prize, backward reading: who grumbles if white writers win awards?', 'Why the TS Eliot prize shortlist hails a return to the status quo', 'Forward poetry prizes announce trailblazing shortlists,' etc).

But of course, *none of this has anything to do with poetry*. British cultural life has *always* been distorted by vested interests, social class, geography and political quietism, dominated by social groups wholly unrepresentative of British society and untypical of most people who read and write poetry. Until recently cultural privilege defended its investments behind words like 'tradition', 'standards' and 'taste'. In the absence of an agreed vocabulary for discussing poetry every prize-winning collection is 'bold,' 'dark,' 'sassy,' 'daring,' 'honest,' 'audacious,' 'authentic,' 'personal' and 'brave'. These days power has to dress up in democratic rags in order to get what it wants and to keep what it already possesses.

When a few years ago the Poetry Book Society announced the 'Next Generation Poets' it was with the usual fanfare of self-congratulation and wild applause. The poets involved in the promotion were the 'most exciting new poets from the UK and Ireland'. Not only are they 'doing something new,' 'tackling fresh subject matter,' taking 'emotional and literary risks', and 'reinvigorating the poetry scene', these poets are 'expected to dominate the poetry landscape of the coming decade' and lead 'our national cultural conversation for many years to come.' People who make fatuous claims about 'dominating the poetry landscape' should remember Auden's reminder that it is the responsibility of poets 'to defend the language against corruption,' otherwise 'people lose faith in what they hear'.

British literary life would certainly be a little less dull if real cultural power (not just the composition of competition judging panels) were more widely diffused. Personally, I would like to see more working-class poets in print, fewer critics who have been to university, more publishers based outside London, and fewer poets with Creative Writing MAs. But this is not, I think, what calls for greater diversity usually mean.

The *Guardian* recently brought us the exciting news that 'a passion for politics, particularly among teenagers and young millennials, is fuelling a dramatic growth in the popularity of poetry.' This followed on from the announcement in the paper a few months earlier that poetry is now 'the coolest thing' and that 'young rebel poets' from the 'emerging underground' are at last 'breaking the mould of traditional, more elitist verse'. Of the three 'young rebel poets' from the 'underground poetry scene' acclaimed by the *Guardian*, one was a beneficiary of the Poetry Society's Next Generation promotion and short-listed for the Costa Prize; one has been published by Penguin; the other is published by Simon and Schuster.

There are a great many poets writing today whose work might properly be described as rebellious or underground. But they are not very likely to be recognised by the gate-keepers at the *Guardian* or *Poetry Review*.

Smokestack Books was established in 2004 with the explicit

THE PRIVATISATION OF POETRY

intention of publishing oppositional, dissident, unfashionable and radical poets. Smokestack's declared aim is to keep open a space for what is left of the socialist and communist poetic traditions in the twenty-first century, publishing books that otherwise would be unlikely to appear in print, and putting into English poets whose work is either unavailable or unknown in the UK.

To date Smokestack has published 160 titles and over 44k books, including John Berger's *Collected Poems*, two collections for grown-ups by Michael Rosen, the collected lyrics of Victor Jara, two book-length poems by Yiannis Ritsos, Paul van Ostaijen's anti-war Dadaist epic *Occupied City*, and anthologies of poetry from Palestine, Cuba, Siberia, the USA, France and Algeria. Smokestack poets include Linda France, Katrina Porteous, Martin Rowson, Ian McMillan, Kate Fox, Sebastian Barker, Judith Kazantzis, Martin Hayes, Gerda Stevenson and Steve Ely.

Smokestack's international list includes books by Vladimir Mayakovsky (Soviet Union), Bertolt Brecht (Germany), Gustavo Pereira (Venezuela), Guus Luijters (Netherlands), Francis Combes (France), Rocco Scotellaro (Italy), Heinrich Heine (Germany), Nikola Vaptsarov (Bulgaria), Andras Mezei (Hungary), Jim Scully (US), Justyna Bargielska (Poland), Louis Aragon (France), Jan Carew (Guyana), Ghassan Zaqtan (Palestine), Jack Lindsay (Australia), Frank Reeve (US), Amir Darwish (Syria), Martín Espada (Puerto Rico/US), Reja-e Busailah (Palestine), Goran Simic (Bosnia) and Roque Dalton (El Salvador). Three Smokestack books have won PEN Translation awards. Two have been translated into Italian and one into Turkish. Smokestack was recently shortlisted for the Small Press of the Year award.

Smokestack titles are often intended as specific *interventions*, contributions to a conversation about a particular issue – for example, Mayakovsky's epic poem *Lenin* (the centenary of 1917), Dinos Siotis (ed) *Crisis* (the Greek economic and political crisis), David Betteridge (ed) *A Rose Loupt Oot* (the fortieth anniversary of the UCS work-in), Amir Darwish's *Dear Refugee* and *Don't Forget the Couscous* (the Syrian refugee crisis), Tom Wintringham's *We're Going*

On! (the seventieth anniversary of the beginning of the Spanish Civil War), David Cain's *Truth Street* (the thirtieth anniversary of the Hillsborough disaster), Bill Herbert and Andy Jackson (eds) *New Boots and Pantisocracies* (the first 100 days of the Cameron government) and two sequences about Brexit – John Gohorry's *Squeak, Budgie!* and Martin Rowson's *Pastrami Faced Racist.*

Andras Mezei's *Christmas in Auschwitz*, Thomas Ország-Land (ed) *Survivors: Hungarian Jewish Poets of the Holocaust* and Guus Luijters' *Song of Stars* were published in response to the rise of neo-Fascism and anti-Semitism in Europe. A percentage of the sales of Naomi Foyle (ed) *A Blade of Grass: New Palestinian Poetry* goes towards the legal fees of Ashraf Fayadh and Dareen Tatour, Palestinian poets currently imprisoned in Saudi Arabia and Israel on charges relating to their poetry.

Smokestack has always been interested in publishing poets who are writing a long way from the metropolitan centres of cultural authority, like Martin Hayes (who works in a London courier office), John Tait (a postman), Karl Riordan (a disability support worker) and Ross Wilson (an auxiliary nurse). Gordon Hodgeon wrote his last two Smokestack books from his hospital bed, the first using voice-recognition software, the second by blinking at a computer-screen.

This is not, I think, a project entirely lacking in interest, distinction – or radicalism. But of course, no Smokestack title has ever been noticed by the *Guardian*. Only three have ever been reviewed in *Poetry Review*. Smokestack does not receive any public subsidy. *This is not a complaint. And it is certainly not a surprise.* British literary life has always been an unwelcoming, unfriendly and uncomradely place. There are many reasons why only three Smokestack titles have ever been reviewed in *Poetry Review*, but they have nothing to do with poetry. Anyway, Smokestack was set up in order to oppose the ideological values and cultural assumptions that ignore most poets, most poems and most people most of the time. There are many poetry worlds; the Poetry Society represents just one of them.

Poetry does not need a 'revival' any more than jumping does, or whistling or humming or giggling. Poetry is not cool; it is necessary. It is neither a talent-contest nor an industry. And it has nothing to do with the values of show-business or big-business, corporate PR or copyright law. The importance of poetry is not calculated in sales-figures, and its value is not measured by prizes. Poetry cannot be owned because it already belongs to anyone and everyone.

Among the writers at the al-Marbed festival in Basra was the Iraqi poet Chawki Abdelamir. Stripped of his citizenship in the 1970s, Chawki lived for many years in Algiers, Beirut and Paris (where he was the cultural attaché for the South Yemeni government). He is currently the Iraqi representative on UNESCO. Chawki has translated Gullevic into Arabic, Adonis into French, and published over 30 books, most recently *Attenter à la mort*, which Smokestack is publishing in English next year

> I live in the Baghdad National Library
> a blind seer
> between lines of ash
> I touch the text's carbon
> like a child stroking the head
> of his dying father
>
> The office chair
> is a skeleton with blackened limbs
> scrumpling a still white
> sheet of paper
>
> From the window
> stripped naked by the flames
> a dishevelled palm tree stands
> reciting hymns
> from the index of lost titles
> and great chapters of the history of fire
> in the parchment of Baghdad
>
> I went out
> clutching my pen

— *PN Review*, 247, May-June 2019

SMOKESTACK LIGHTNING

In *A Poetry Inferno* by the late John Hartley Williams, a poet reads a translation of Proust in rhyming couplets to a small audience condemned to sit on hard chairs for so long they have turned to stone. It's a vision of hell – one of the infernal circles in a very funny take on the contemporary poetry scene. In the First Circle (Magazine Submission Hell), poets wait for ever for a rejection letter. In the Second Circle (Anthology Hell), they must spend eternity stabbing each other in the back. Poets who have given up writing 'in order to talk about it' can be found in the Fourth Circle (Writers' Block Hell), while in the Sixth Circle (Laureate Hell), poetry professors and prize-winners are executed for betraying their vocation. In the Seventh Circle (Ignoramus Hell) 'a meandering torrent of brown filth stretches into the distance, and along its banks, flailed onward by devils with nine-tailed lashes, go lines of tiny figures' marching into Dante's arse.

The UK poetry world often seems a ridiculous, embarrassing and unfriendly place. The exchange and dissemination of poetry is increasingly policed by the values of show business and big business, and public conversations about poetry are often unkind, uncomradely and ungenerous. For all the current talk of diversity, the poetry world still seems determined to alienate as many people as possible. The language of the bouncers at the door may change, but you still need to show your invitation to get in.

Smokestack Books was established in 2004 in protest at the dullness, narrowness and triviality of so much of the contemporary British poetry scene. Smokestack's declared aim has always been to keep open a space for what is left of the radical poetic tradition in the twenty-first century:

Smokestack champions poets who are unfashionable, radical, left-field and working a long way from the metropolitan centres of cultural authority. Smokestack is interested in the World as well as the Word; believes that poetry is a part of and not apart from society; argues that if poetry does not belong to everyone it is not poetry.

Since then, Smokestack has published two hundred titles and sold well over 50k books, and has twice been long-listed for the British Book Awards Small Press of the Year. Five Smokestack titles have won PEN Translation awards. Two have recently been translated into Italian, and one into Turkish.

This book is an opportunity to look back on the distance covered so far. There are 199 poems here, one from each of the books that Smokestack has published, including poems from Algeria, Australia, Bosnia, Bulgaria, Chile, Cuba, El Salvador, France, Germany, Greece, Guyana, Hungary, Iraq, Italy, the Netherlands, Palestine, Poland, Russia/Soviet Union, Spain, Syria, the USA and Venezuela.

Like any good anthology, it's a noisy collection, baggy and bulging and contradictory, pulling in different directions. These poems were never intended to be inside the same covers. A few have been overtaken by events. Others look a little lonely without the context or the support of the sequences in which they were first published. None of the accompanying photographs, drawings, illustrations and cartoons are included here. Poems that originally appeared in two languages are represented only in translation.

Nevertheless, all these poets may be said to inhabit a shared seriousness, and a common preparedness to write about the circumstances in which they found themselves. This is what Brecht meant when he talked about 'singing in the dark times'. Many of these books were published as specific interventions, contributions to the public conversation around a particular issue – the centenary of 1917, the Greek economic and political crisis, the fortieth anniversary of the UCS work-in, the seventieth anniversaries of the beginning of the Spanish Civil War and the end of the Second World War, the refugee crisis, Brexit, the thirtieth anniversary of the Hillsborough disaster, the COVID pandemic, the rise of neo-Fascism and anti-Semitism in Europe, the struggle of the Palestinian people for statehood.

There are many different – and sometimes competing – intellectual and political loyalties represented in these pages. But the anthology is predicated on the belief that poetry is a social production or it is nothing at all; that it is a way of exercising citizenship and demonstrating belonging; that it can be a means of knowing ourselves and others better, of sharing and extending the common ownership of experience, feeling and language, of resisting the forces that would divide us. Poetry is one of the ways in which competing common-senses can be articulated, reinforced and challenged. A poem can bear witness, clarify ideas and articulate an emotional line of march. A poem can describe the world as it is and at the same time show us how it might be. And as Francis Combes observes in 'Utilité de la poesie', poetry can be necessary, beautiful *and* useful:

> A young beggar seen in the Metro
> had written these words
> on a piece of cardboard hung round his neck:
> 'As the burning forest
> shouts towards the river's water
> I appeal to you:
> Please give me
> something to eat.'
> And it seems
> People were giving.
> (Which would tend to point to
> the usefulness of poetry
> in our societies.)

— Introduction to *Smokestack Lightning*
(Smokestack Books, 2021)

BROWNING'S UNDERPANTS AND THE UGLY SISTERS

A few months ago, the editor of Poetry Review shared with members of the Poetry Society a disturbing dream in which he had found himself defending the state of contemporary poetry against a 'National Treasure and Public Intellectual'. With his shirt buttoned up tight, his neatly combed hair and his 'little badge of cultural influence', this nightmarish figure seemed intent on reducing poetry to a series of cartoon museum pieces, like artefacts in glass cabinets: 'Keats' death mask, the cigarette ash of Auden, the underpants of Robert Browning.'

It was an interesting way of dramatizing a supposed internal argument between poets about Ancients and Moderns. But alarming that it involved identifying contemporary poetry as being somehow in opposition to the idea of the public literary intellectual. Raymond Williams once pointed out that uses of the word 'intellectual' in English have historically been associated with hostile ideas about elitism. While it would be hard to write a history of, say, France or Russia without attending to the role of the literary intelligentsia, their dynamic and changing relationship to power and to society, it would be much easier to write a history of anti-intellectual resentments in Britain. But these resentments have not, hitherto, been located in the world of poetry. And poets have not always been so far removed from public discourse.

Terry Eagleton observed a few years ago that 'for almost the first time in two centuries, there is no eminent British poet prepared to question the foundations of the Western way of life'. But who are the 'eminent' poets of our time? Who gets to decide? (And what kind of critical term is 'eminence'?) Eagleton needs to get out a bit more. British poets have arguably never been more concerned to interrogate the way we live, than at present. *But how would anyone know?* Where are the places where serious readers and serious writers can meet? Where are the conversations about poetry rather than poets? And anyway, who is listening?

At a time of deepening structural inequalities in British life, poets are hidden behind university walls, competing for prizes and commissions, protected by agents, copyright lawyers and exaggerated claims for the importance of poetry. (According to the *Guardian,* during the COVID pandemic 'almost everyone' found themselves 'turning to poetry', while for *Vanity Fair* poetry enjoyed 'a bump in cultural relevance as the world sits at home and considers its surroundings...')

The gate-keepers who control access to the world of poetry – the broadsheets, the Arts Council, the BBC, book-festivals, prize-giving foundations, the Poetry Society – also isolate it from the world and inoculate it against controversy. When a few years ago Merryn Wiliams (ed) *Poems for Jeremy Corbyn* was launched at the Labour Party conference, the broadsheets were quick to ridicule it as 'fan poetry' and 'doggerel'; one Blairite MP told the *Daily Telegraph* that the book was 'the only thing that had made him smile all week'. A few years ago, when I suggested that the Poetry Society might host a debate about the 'Plagiarism' controversies, the idea was turned down on the grounds that it was too 'controversial'. When I recently offered *Poetry News* a short history of Smokestack Books it was rejected because it wasn't '*positive*' enough; they wanted to know how much '*fun*' it was working with so many '*amazing*' poets.

In the last twenty years the poetry-reading circuit has collapsed into a culture of slams and open mics. Adult education writing workshops have been replaced by HE Creative Writing programmes. Local poetry festivals have been swallowed by corporate book festivals. *Kaleidoscope* by *Front Row.* Poets who used to work in community writing residencies have disappeared onto university campuses. Yesterday's elitists are today's Populists. In place of the critical culture of small magazines and poetry presses, we have life-style profiles of poets in the weeklies. Although these days the *Guardian* reviews new poetry only sporadically, in the last ten years the paper has published *over seventy* reviews, features and interviews with Kae Tempest. And every poet must have a prize.

As the poet Martin Hayes has put it, the poetry world is 'full of ugly sisters running around trying to find the glass slipper to wedge their ugly foot into so that they can then run around saying, "Look at me! Look at me! I'm the one!"'

After leaving school at 15, Martin Hayes worked as a leaflet distributor, accounts clerk, courier, telephonist, recruitment manager and a control room supervisor for a courier firm in London. He has also published seven books of poetry, mostly about work. This is unusual. People don't work very much in contemporary poetry:

> 'as we allocated out the thousands of jobs
> trying to keep it safe and tidy
> so that we could protect our minds and dignity
> from the supervisors who would come out
> every time they caught us fucking up
> and try to strip it all away
> by screaming and shouting at us
> that we were 'idiots'
> and 'fucking morons'
> poets are writing about the shadows tulips cast in distilling light
> and what help does that give us!
>
> as we spoke to customers
> whose jobs hadn't been picked up on time
> whose lives now will never be the same
> trying to appease them by using our street learned charm
> sweet talking them with our treacle tongues
> convincing them that this was a one off
> that will most certainly never happen again madam
>
> poets are writing about their sexuality
> and how hard it is coming to terms with it
> and what help does that give us!
> as we tried to manage the couriers' needs
> tried to convince them that we were not there
> just to stitch them up
> but were just trying to do our job
> because we also had our rent to be paid
> and our electricity bill to be paid
> and our council tax to pay for
> and our county court judgements to pay for

> poets are writing about oak trees and how a bowl of fruit
> left for a week on one of their 5-grand breakfast tables
> gives off a scent that reminds them of their childhood
> and what help does that give us!

Four of Hayes' books were published by Smokestack Books, examples of Smokestack's attempt to break out of poetry's self-imposed isolation by bringing together serious readers and serious writers around serious issues, especially the relationship between writing and society, action and words, responsibility and complicity. To nudge the dial, as they say.

Smokestack was also a protest at the terminal dullness of so much of the contemporary UK poetry scene, its self-importance, excitability, lack of seriousness and self-imposed isolation from the rest of society. Smokestack's models were Curbstone Press in the US and Le Temps des Cerises in France, publishers of 'la poésie d'utilité publique'.

In twenty years, Smokestack sold over 65k books and published 237 titles. Smokestack poets included John Berger, Michael Rosen, Sylvia Pankhurst, Vernon Scannell, Linda France, Bill Herbert, Katrina Porteous, Ian McMillan, Kate Fox, Sebastian Barker, Judith Kazantzis, John Lucas, Martin Rowson, Gerda Stevenson and Steve Ely.

Smokestack's international list included books by Victor Jara (Chile), Yiannis Ritsos and Tasos Leivaditis (Greece), Vladimir Mayakovsky, Ilya Ehrenburg, Olga Berggholts, Konstantin Simonov and Alexandr Tvardovsky (Soviet Union), Bertolt Brecht, Heinrich Heine and Volker Braun (Germany), Gustavo Pereira (Venezuela), Guus Luijters (Netherlands), Louis Aragon and Francis Combes (France), Rocco Scotellaro and Laura Fusco (Italy), Nikola Vaptsarov (Bulgaria), Andras Mezei (Hungary), Justyna Bargielska (Poland), Jan Carew (Guyana), Ghassan Zaqtan and Tawfiq Zayyad (Palestine), Jack Lindsay (Australia), Martín Espada, Fred Voss, Jim Scully, Larry Beckett and Frank Reeve (USA), Amir Darwish (Syria), Goran Simic (Bosnia), Chawki Abdelamir (Iraq), Roque Dalton (El Salvador), Paul van

Ostaijen (Belgium), Anna Greki (Algeria), Ilhan Comak (Turkey), and anthologies of poetry from Cuba, Siberia, the USA, Greece, Kurdistan, Hungary, the Soviet Union, France, Algeria, Kurdistan and Palestine.

Julia Nemirovskaya (ed) *Disbelief: 100 Russian Anti-war Poems* was the first bilingual collection of anti-war poems by Russian writers published anywhere in the world after the Russian invasion of Ukraine. Atef Alshaer and Alan Morrison (eds) *Out of Gaza: New Palestinian Poetry* was published just three months after the Israeli invasion of Gaza, to raise money for the Palestine Solidarity Campaign. Ilhan Comak's *Separated from the Sun* was published to raise public awareness about its author, who has been in a Turkish prison since 1994 for the crime of Kurdish 'separatism'.

In its way, Smokestack was a small success story, putting into print poets who might otherwise not have been published and introducing to UK readers those whose work was hitherto unavailable in English. And yet, it always felt as though Smokestack titles were published in silence, in secret, *samizdat.* After twenty years, Smokestack titles still struggled to make themselves heard above the victory march of the Next Big Thing. No Smokestack title was ever reviewed in the *Guardian*. Only three Smokestack titles were reviewed in *Poetry Review*. Only one was ever featured on *The Verb*. It always felt as though no-one was listening. The dial didn't budge. The ugly sisters are still arguing about Browning's underpants.

— *PN Review 280*, December 2024

ACKNOWLEDGEMENTS

Thanks are due to the editors of the books, newspapers, magazines and websites where these essays were first published. I have tidied and edited some of them, mostly to avoid repetition, and thus accusations of self-plagiarism. Thanks too, to Jonathan Davidson and Mark Robinson for their encouragement and comments on early drafts of this book.

LAY OUT YOUR UNREST

Milton Keynes UK
Ingram Content Group UK Ltd.
UKHW031441071124
450868UK00005B/85

9 781916 938670